The Layperson's Distinctive Role

FRANCIS CARDINAL ARINZE

The Layperson's Distinctive Role

IGNATIUS PRESS   SAN FRANCISCO

Cover photograph: © iStockPhoto.com
Cover design by John Herreid

© 2013 by Ignatius Press, San Francisco
All rights reserved
ISBN 978-1-58617-780-5
Library of Congress Control Number 2013938208
Printed in the United States of America ∞

Contents

Introduction

In preparation for the founding of his Church, our Lord Jesus Christ gathered followers. He had a close group of twelve Apostles. These he trained in a special way. At the end of his public ministry, he gave them the Holy Spirit, ordained them bishops, as we would say today, and commissioned and sent them, under the leadership of Peter, to look after his Church in his name. After Christ ascended into heaven, the Apostles, the first bishops, chose and ordained helpers, who came with time to be known as priests (presbyters) and deacons. These clerics are ordained to minister to all the rest of the people of God. The word "laity" is from the Greek word *laos*, "people". The religious or consecrated life as we know it today arose in the Church in the third century, with Saint Anthony of Egypt (c. 251–355) as one of the earliest monks. This book is about the apostolate of the lay faithful in the Church and in the world.

It is important for all in the Church to have a good understanding of the apostolate specific to the laity. The Second Vatican Council (1962–1965) contributed much in this direction, especially in its major document, the Dogmatic Constitution on the Church *Lumen Gentium* and its Decree on the Apostolate of the Laity *Apostolicam Actuositatem*. Blessed John Paul II, after the 1987 Synod of Bishops on the topic "The Vocation and Mission of the Lay Faithful in the

Church and in the World", issued the Post-synodal Apostolic Exhortation *Christifideles Laici* in 1988. These three documents provide the major orientation for our times on the role of the lay faithful in the Church and in the world.

This present book focuses on what is distinctive about the lay apostolate. To lay the groundwork, a brief reflection is made on the call of every baptized person to the apostolate, on the nature of the lay apostolate and on the various forms in which the lay role can be expressed. The central message of this book is in the fifth consideration: the specific role of the laity.

In order to think more deeply about the role of the laity, reasons are given for the urgency of lay initiative, together with what it has de facto achieved in some countries. There are, however, reasons why some clerics and even lay faithful are doubtful about the wisdom of the laity assuming a distinctive role. These reasons need to be addressed. It is important to have a clear idea of the different roles in the Church and to formulate a sound and dynamic theology of the laity and also of their spirituality.

Recent ecclesial movements, communities and institutes will also be examined, because of their growing importance in the Church and in the world today. A word on the need for formation will bring these reflections to an end.

Every Baptized Person
Is Called to Evangelize

When our beloved Lord and Savior Jesus Christ was inaugurating the Kingdom of God, he called people to come after him. "Follow me" is the invitation he gave to his first disciples (Mt 4:19; Mk 1:17; Lk 5:27; Jn 1:43). After the death and Resurrection of Christ, the new religion was called the "Way" (Acts 9:2). It was later in Antioch that "the disciples were for the first time called Christians" (Acts 11:26).

After the first disciples had followed Jesus for some time, he sent not only the twelve Apostles to preach (Mt 10:1) but also the seventy-two disciples. Of these latter, the evangelist Luke says that Jesus "sent them on ahead of him, two by two, into every town and place where he himself was about to come. And he said to them, 'The harvest is plentiful, but the laborers are few; pray therefore the Lord of the harvest to send out laborers into his harvest'" (Lk 10:1−2).

In the Sermon on the Mount, Jesus was speaking to all his followers when he likened them to salt and light: "You are the salt of the earth. . . . You are the light of the world. . . . Let your light so shine before men, that they may see your good works and give glory to your Father who is in heaven" (Mt 5:13, 14, 16).

Saint Paul tells the Corinthians that the Holy Spirit gives different gifts to various people in the Church for the common good: "There are varieties of gifts, but the same Spirit;

and there are varieties of service, but the same Lord. . . . To each is given the manifestation of the Spirit for the common good" (1 Cor 12:4-5, 7).

Just before Jesus went back to heaven, he sent the Apostles, and through them the whole Church, to evangelize: "You shall be my witnesses in Jerusalem and in all Judea and Samaria and to the end of the earth" (Acts 1:8). And in case anyone suspects that the call to witness to Christ is really directed to the clerics and not so much to the laity, Jesus had earlier declared: "Every one who acknowledges me before men, the Son of man also will acknowledge before the angels of God; but he who denies me before men will be denied before the angels of God" (Lk 12:8-9).

The Church has therefore always understood the call to follow Christ by faith and Baptism as a call to the apostolate. By apostolate, we mean the mission of the Church, the motive of Christ in founding his Church. It is to spread the Good News of salvation in Jesus Christ, so that all men and women may know the one true God and Jesus Christ whom he has sent and, by knowing him, believe in him, live the new life he has won for all mankind and find eternal salvation in his name. This mission, declares the Second Vatican Council, the Church carries out through all her members. "For by its very nature the Christian vocation is also a vocation to the apostolate. No part of the structure of a living body is merely passive but each has a share in the functions as well as in the life of the body. . . . Indeed, so intimately are the parts linked and interrelated in this body (cf. Eph. 4:16) that the member who fails to make his proper contribution to the development of the Church must be said to be useful neither to the Church nor to himself."[1] There are

---

[1] Vatican II, Decree on the Apostolate of the Laity *Apostolicam Actuositatem*, 2. Unless otherwise noted, all quotations from Vatican II documents are from *The Documents of Vatican II*, ed. Walter M. Abbott, S.J. (America

no spectators in the Church. The apostolate is not like soccer, where twenty-two people are playing and twenty-two million are watching, cheering, yelling or booing! Everyone in the Church has a role to play.

Everyone in the Church shares in the Church's mission according to each person's vocation. There are three major categories of vocations in the Church. Those who have received Holy Orders—bishops, priests and deacons—are called to gather the people of God together for public worship and to sanctify them by preaching the word of God and administering the sacraments. Consecrated people are called to live by the three evangelical counsels of chastity, poverty and obedience and thus to show that the Kingdom of God and its ultimate necessities are superior to all earthly considerations. The lay faithful, the vast majority of the members of the Church—indeed, 99.9 percent of her members[2]— are called by Baptism to witness to Christ in the secular sphere of life, that is, in the family; in work and leisure; in science and culture; in politics and government; in trade and mass media; and in national and international relations. Their specific apostolate is the main concern of this book.

Press, 1966), and all other Church documents are quoted from the Vatican website.

[2] According to the March 2012 *Statistical Yearbook of the Church*, there were 1,195,671,000 Catholics in the world on June 30, 2010. On December 31, 2010, there were a total of 1,196,000,000 Catholics, of whom bishops numbered 5,104, priests 412,236, religious women 721,935, and religious men (not priests) 54,665. Therefore, the lay faithful numbered 1,194,806,060, or 99.9 percent of the whole Catholic Church. See *Statistical Yearbook of the Church*, March 2012, pp. 17, 77; also *Avvenire*, 11/3/2012, p. 24.

2

The Nature of the Lay Apostolate

Mission follows on vocation. The apostolate expected of a person in the Church depends on and follows on what that person is called to be in the Church. Therefore the proper way to understand the lay apostolate is first to ask who the layperson is.

Many people would likely give a negative definition of the layperson. They would probably say that a layperson is a Christian who is neither a cleric nor a religious. Such a definition is insufficient. Even good logic requires that a definition not be a negative statement if it can be a positive one. And in this case it can, and should, be positive. How would a diocesan priest like to be defined as a Christian who is neither a layperson nor a religious? A definition is important because it hits at what is considered most essential regarding the defined thing, person, group or concept.

The Fathers of the Second Vatican Council go about the definition of the laity rather carefully in paragraph 31 of the Dogmatic Constitution on the Church, *Lumen Gentium*. They begin with a brief negative description in order to make clear about whom they are speaking, to demarcate the lines, so to speak. They describe the term "laity" as here understood to mean all the faithful except those in Holy Orders and those in a religious state. Then the Fathers of the Council move positively to tell us that the laity are those who by Baptism are made one body with Christ and incorporated into the Church. They have a share in Christ, who is priest, prophet and king. They carry out their own part in the mission of the whole Church by engaging in temporal affairs and ordering them according to the plan of God. They live in the world, that is, in each and in all of the secular professions and occupations, in the ordinary circumstances of family and social life "from which the very web of their existence is woven".

The Council continues by adding that this means that a secular character is specific to the vocation and mission of the laity. They are called to "work for the sanctification of the world from within in the manner of leaven". It is the responsibility of the laity to illuminate and organize temporal affairs (family, work, leisure, politics, government, trade, science and technology) "in such a way that they may always start out, develop, and persist according to Christ's mind, and to the praise of the Creator and Redeemer".[1]

Now we have a positive and dynamic definition of the layperson: one who by Baptism is incorporated into Christ and the Church and is called to evangelize the secular order. Blessed John Paul II calls on the lay faithful to realize the height and depth of their vocation: "Only through accepting the richness in the mystery that God gives to the Christian in Baptism is it possible to come to a basic description of the lay faithful. . . . Baptism regenerates us in the life of the Son of God; unites us to Christ and to his Body, the Church; and anoints us in the Holy Spirit, making us spiritual temples."[2]

The Second Vatican Council therefore dedicates the Decree *Apostolicam Actuositatem* to explaining the apostolate of the lay faithful and to urging the laity to be generous in wit-

---

[1] Vatican II, Dogmatic Constitution on the Church *Lumen Gentium*, 31.
[2] John Paul II, Post-synodal Apostolic Exhortation *Christifideles Laici*, 9, 10.

nessing to Christ. In the concluding paragraph, the Council Fathers declare: "The Council, then, earnestly entreats in the Lord that all laymen give a glad, generous, and prompt response to the voice of Christ, who is giving them an especially urgent invitation at this moment, and to the impulse of the Holy Spirit."[3]

[3] Vatican II, Decree on the Apostolate of Lay People *Apostolicam Actuositatem*, 33.

3

The Lay Apostolate
in the New Testament

In order to deepen our understanding of the lay apostolate, it is helpful to recall some examples of Christian witness from the New Testament. There we see that some of the first witnesses to Christ did not belong to the priestly class.

The Virgin Mary and Saint Joseph are in a special category. We may not call them laity in the technical sense of today, but we can observe that Joseph, a carpenter, was not a religious leader. We cannot but admire the wonderful way in which he and Mary carried out the singular roles assigned to them by Divine Providence. In mostly ordinary circumstances and among ordinary people, they fulfilled their part in God's plan for the Incarnation and Redemption.

Simeon and the widow Anna, although not strictly laypeople since the Church was not yet founded, did not belong to the Jewish priestly class. They gave witness to the newborn Savior, "a light for revelation to the Gentiles, and for glory to your people Israel" (Lk 2:32). The Samaritan woman, herself not yet a Christian and certainly not a saint, brought her fellow Samaritans to recognize Jesus as "the Savior of the world" by her witness (Jn 4:42). The Gerasene demoniac, out of whom Jesus cast a legion of devils, begged Jesus to be allowed to be one of his "full-time" followers (today we might say he wanted to enter the seminary). But Jesus refused and instead sent him home to engage in the lay apostolate. Jesus said to him: "Go home to your friends, and tell them how much the Lord has done for you, and how he has had mercy on you." The text continues: "And he went away and began to proclaim in the Decapolis how much Jesus had done for him; and all men marveled" (Mk 5:19–20). This is very eloquent.

Mary Magdalene, out of whom seven devils were cast (Lk 8:2), followed Jesus and was one of the women who supplied him and his Apostles with some material needs. She was courageous enough to be on Calvary. She returned to the tomb on Easter Day and was thus privileged to see the risen Christ, who sent her to bring the Good News of his Resurrection to the Apostles (Jn 20:11–18). Saint Thomas Aquinas calls her "the apostle of the Apostles".[1]

In the Acts of the Apostles the centurion Cornelius brought his whole household to Baptism (Acts 10). In Antioch the early followers of Christ were so fervent that "the disciples were for the first time called Christians" (Acts 11:26). Dionysius the Areopagite and a woman called Damaris responded positively to Saint Paul's speech in Athens and hopefully influenced others (Acts 17:34). Saint Paul in his letters mentions such "fellow workers" in the Gospel as Apollos, Aquila, Priscilla, Euodia, Syntyche, Clement, Aristarchus, Luke, Demas, Epaphras, Nympha and many others (Acts 18:24, 26; Phil 2:25; 4:2–3; Col 4:10–16; Rom 16:9; Philem 24).

We can also add that laypeople soon after the apostolic age gave wonderful witness to Christ, and many laid down their lives for him. The Roman Canon of the Mass (Eucharistic Prayer I) commemorates such valiant martyrs as Cosmas and

---

[1] *In Joannem evang. expositio* 20.3.6; cf. also Rabanus Maurus, *De vita beatae Mariae Magdalenae* 27, PL 112:1474, and John Paul II, Apostolic Letter *Mulieris Dignitatem*, 16.

Damian (medical doctors); John and Paul (court officials at the time of Julian the Apostate); Felicity and Perpetua (the former a pregnant woman, the latter a twenty-two-year-old mother with a baby at the breast, both from Carthage in North Africa), Agatha; Lucy; Agnes; Cecilia; and Anastasia.

It therefore shines out from the New Testament and from the days of the early Church that the lay faithful have not been lacking but have fully participated in giving witness to Christ, as Saint Peter exhorts the early Christians: "Always be prepared to make a defense to any one who calls you to account for the hope that is in you" (1 Pet 3:15).

4

Variety in Forms of the Lay Apostolate

Situations, problems and challenges that exist in the Church around the world vary greatly indeed. For this reason, the ways in which the lay apostolate expresses itself are many. Generalizations and oversimplifications should be avoided.

Some lay apostolate undertakings have the broad apostolic purpose of the Church in view. Others aim at the evangelization inspired by a particular spirituality. Some intend simply to collaborate with the clergy in inner-Church affairs. Some bear witness to Christ in a particular way through works of mercy and charity. Others propose to infuse a Christian spirit into the temporal order or to animate particular professional groups.[1] A little reflection on each of these will make these general remarks clearer.

Lay apostolate: Individual and organized

The laity can exercise their apostolate as individuals or as members of organized groups. Every layperson can, and should, give witness to Christ as an individual parent, doctor, lawyer, teacher, business owner, nurse, taxi driver, pilot, politician, etc. There are situations in which an organized lay apostolate is not easy or even possible, as is the case under

[1] See *Apostolicam Actuositatem*, 19.

oppressive regimes, in times of revolution or war and during periods of religious persecution. The individual apostolate "admits of no substitute" and "is the origin and condition of the whole lay apostolate", says the Second Vatican Council.[2] There are many things that individual laypeople can accomplish for Christ and his Gospel singlehandedly, quietly and without any external organization or association with others.

Nevertheless, organization eventually becomes necessary in the lay apostolate because some problems and challenges surpass the capacity of one individual to meet them adequately. Think of the forces that militate against marriage and the family or promote abortion and euthanasia in legislative bodies. There are political parties that demand of their candidates support for contraception, abortion and other practices contrary to a properly formed Christian conscience. There are states where Catholic schools are seized by the government, where immigration laws separate family members and undermine solidarity and where there is little or no provision for financial relief for families with many children. Then there are major questions on war, justice and peace. These and similar problems and challenges call for organized and joint action by the lay faithful if they are to be adequately tackled. "It can be helpful for you to form associations in order to continue shaping your Christian conscience and supporting one another in the struggle for justice and peace", Pope Benedict XVI told the laypeople in Africa.[3] It has been traditional in the Church to have organized forms of the lay apostolate in parishes, dioceses or

---

[2] Ibid., 16.
[3] Benedict XVI, Post-synodal Apostolic Exhortation *Africae Munus*, 131.

countries and sometimes also at the world level. Some such organizations will be considered later in this book.

Among the other reasons why organized lay apostolates are sometimes necessary are the social nature of the human being and, even more important, the nature of the Church as communion. Jesus has told us: "Where two or three are gathered in my name, there am I in the midst of them" (Mt 18:20). Moreover, the pooling of resources can achieve more than an individual can hope to achieve. One should also not forget the international level in a world that is behaving more and more like a global village: "In view of the progress of social institutions and the fast-moving pace of modern society, the global nature of the Church's mission requires that apostolic enterprises of Catholics should increasingly develop organized forms at the international level."[4] Such organizations help to "form an awareness of genuine universal solidarity and responsibility".[5] In 2007 the Pontifical Council for the Laity published a directory, *International Associations of the Faithful*, listing 122 groups to which it has given approval at the universal level.

Laypeople's collaboration in inner-Church affairs

By Baptism the laity are incorporated into Christ and the Church and become sharers in Christ as priest, prophet and king. They have therefore a part to play also in the inner

[4] *Apostolicam Actuositatem*, 19.

[5] Vatican II, Pastoral Constitution on the Church in the Modern World *Gaudium et Spes*, 90.

life and activity of the Church. The Second Vatican Council is clear: "Their activity is so necessary within church communities that without it the apostolate of the pastors is generally unable to achieve its full effectiveness."[6]

Think of all the parish activities that rely upon the involvement of the laity: faith formation programs, Bible studies, preparation classes for the reception of the sacraments, services for the poor and needy, fundraising and building projects. On the diocesan level laypersons are needed to fund, organize and staff schools, charities and outreach ministries. Also needing support are the seminary, vocation awareness programs and newspaper, radio and television projects. Certain challenges or problems call for consultation with the laity. For example, Catholic laypeople can study the question of fees in Catholic educational institutions so that it will not happen that only the richer families are able to send their children to Catholic schools.

Deserving of special mention is the activity of the lay faithful at the college and university levels, whether as presidents, professors, advisers or other staff. The witness of convinced lay academicians is powerful in influencing their fellow laypeople. And benefactors and supporters of Catholic colleges and universities are rendering important contributions to the educational service of the Church.

Beyond the diocese, there are the missionary activities of the universal Church. Laypersons are absolutely vital to the financial and material support of missionary projects, help to the Church under persecution in some parts of the world, support for the Holy Father's universal mission, participation in worldwide lay organizations and the financing of other programs for evangelization.

---

[6] *Apostolicam Actuositatem*, 10.

Every parish priest appreciates the importance of going in search of the lost sheep. Some pastors can speak, not just of one sheep going astray out of a hundred, but of ninety-nine sheep going astray. The priest realizes that it is too little for him to stay in the parish center to look after the one member of the flock that did not drift. And he is convinced that, to search for the lost sheep, he absolutely needs cooperation from the laypeople and the religious in his parish. Many Catholic movements and associations of the laity are very zealous and capable in promoting adult conversions and in encouraging the return of nominal Catholics to full religious practice, complete with frequent Confession and Holy Mass every Sunday. There are Catholic organizations such as the Legion of Mary, the Society of Saint Vincent de Paul, the Knights of Columbus and others that do very praiseworthy work at the grassroots of the Church in the parish. Here we can also mention the basic ecclesial communities that are particularly famous in countries of East Africa.

The participation of the lay faithful in these and other inner-Church affairs remains always important. It is, however, necessary to examine what is most specific to the apostolate of the laity, as will soon become clearer. As Blessed John Paul II puts it, there are two temptations to be avoided in lay participation within the Church: "the temptation of being so strongly interested in Church services and tasks that some fail to become actively engaged in their responsibilities in the professional, social, cultural and political world; and the temptation of legitimizing the unwarranted separation of faith from life, that is, a separation of the Gospel's acceptance from the actual living of the Gospel in various situations in the world".[7]

---

[7] *Christifideles Laici*, 2.

Catholic Action

Particularly in the first half of the twentieth century, in some countries where the Catholic presence was more pronounced, the laity "began to dedicate themselves increasingly to the apostolate. They grouped themselves into various kinds of activities and societies which, in rather close union with the hierarchy, pursued and continue to pursue goals which are properly apostolic."[8] These organizations were approved by the bishops and commended by the popes, and although there were variations in details among them, they were generally called Catholic Action. They were described as collaboration of the laity in the apostolate of the hierarchy and generally possessed four characteristics: their immediate aim was to make the Gospel known and to make people holy; the laity cooperated with the hierarchy by contributing from their own experience; the Church acted as a community; and the laity functioned under the higher direction of the hierarchy.[9]

The Second Vatican Council praised these organizations that went by the name of Catholic Action. The Synod of Bishops that in 1987 discussed the topic "The Vocation and Mission of the Lay Faithful in the Church and in the World" did the same. Blessed John Paul II in the Postsynodal Apostolic Exhortation *Christifideles Laici* in 1988 urged these societies to work in harmony and quoted Saint Paul: "I appeal to you, brethren, by the name of our Lord Jesus Christ, that all of you agree and that there be no dissensions among you, but that you be united in the same

---

[8] *Apostolicam Actuositatem*, 20.
[9] Cf. ibid., 20.

mind and the same judgment" (1 Cor 1:10).[10] In 1991 the
Pontifical Council for the Laity encouraged the setting up of
the International Forum of Catholic Action. The normative
document that this forum worked out was finally approved
by the Pontifical Council in 1995.

The great variety of situations in various countries means
in practice that Catholic Action, so understood, may not suit
all countries. It is not imposed on any country or diocese.
It generally developed in Catholic countries or in countries
where Catholics were a significant percentage of the population and where the custom was for the clergy to give
leadership, not only in inner-Church affairs, but even in sociocultural and political matters. Thus, Catholic Action did
not generally pressure political parties or the government to
make laws in line with the Catholic understanding of natural law. They left such delicate matters to the bishops or to
groups appointed by the bishops.

Lay organizations in more
specifically secular spheres

With the encouragement of the Second Vatican Council and
papal teaching and with the support of bishops and priests,
the lay faithful in the last half century have been developing
more and more ways of witnessing to Christ in the secular sphere. Organizations of Catholic men and women are
getting more directly involved in sociocultural and political matters. Blessed John Paul II reminds the lay faithful
that public life is for everyone and by everyone. Justice demands respect for the rights of people in society. "In order
to achieve their task directed to the Christian animation of

[10] *Christifideles Laici*, 31.

the temporal order, in the sense of serving persons and society, the lay faithful *are never to relinquish their participation in 'public life'*, that is, in the many different economic, social, legislative, administrative and cultural areas, which are intended to promote organically and institutionally the *common good.*"[11]

Pope Benedict XVI distinguished between what the Church is expected to do as Church and what the lay faithful can and should do as Christian citizens. "The Church", he says, "cannot and must not take upon herself the political battle to bring about the most just society possible. She cannot and must not replace the State. Yet at the same time she cannot and must not remain on the sidelines in the fight for justice. She has to play her part through rational argument, and she has to reawaken the spiritual energy without which justice, which always demands sacrifice, cannot prevail and prosper."[12] It is the lay faithful, equipped with dynamic doctrine and fed by the sacraments, who translate involvement in the sociocultural and political matters into reality. "The direct duty to work for a just ordering of society, on the other hand, is proper to the lay faithful. As citizens of the State, they are called to take part in public life in a personal capacity. . . . The mission of the lay faithful is therefore to configure social life correctly, respecting its legitimate autonomy and cooperating with other citizens according to their respective competencies and fulfilling their own responsibility."[13]

This is precisely what the lay apostolate organizations under consideration strive to do. They want to witness to Christ in society, in cultural matters, in political discussion

---

[11] Ibid., 42. Emphasis in original.

[12] Benedict XVI, Encyclical Letter *Deus Caritas Est*, 28.

[13] Ibid., 29.

and in political elections. They join hands to defend the apostolate of the Church in the educational and medical service fields. They do not hesitate to use the press, the internet and radio and television to defend marriage and the family. When necessary, they are able to confront political parties or engage them in dialogue.

Some of these dynamic lay organizations are associations of professionals who are committed to seeing how best they can witness to Christ in society. Thus, we can have the Catholic Medical Association, the Catholic Lawyers Association and the Catholic Business Association. Pope Benedict XVI encouraged such professionals in his Post-synodal Apostolic Exhortation after the Second African Synod: "Lay men and women, in fact, are 'ambassadors of Christ' (2 Cor 5:20) in the public sphere, in the heart of the world. Their Christian witness will be credible only if they are competent and honest professional people."[14] The pope concludes his exhortation to the laity: "I also encourage you to have an active and courageous presence in the areas of political life, culture, the arts, the media and various associations. Do not be hesitant or ashamed about this presence, but be proud of it and conscious of the valuable contribution it can offer to the common good!"[15]

Freedom for laypeople to form or join associations

In view of the great variety among lay apostolate organizations, it is important to allow the laity reasonable freedom. The Second Vatican Council itself insists on this: "As long

[14] *Africae Munus*, 128.
[15] Ibid., 31.

as the proper relationship is kept to Church authorities, the laity have the right to found and run such associations and to join those already existing."[16] Obviously, dissipation of energy, the setting up of rival groups, insistence on associations that have proved themselves overtaken by development and indiscriminate transfer to one country of what is seen to work in another are to be avoided. Moreover, due ecclesiastical approval is needed.

The central point here is that the right of the laity to be involved in the mission of the Church is not a benevolent concession from bishops or priests. The laity have this right and duty by reason of their Baptism. This sacrament creates a fundamental equality among all the baptized: to live the new life in Christ and to witness to him according to one's vocation in the Church and in the world.

It necessarily follows that this right is to be exercised in harmony with the nature of the Church, which is a communion, an organic communion of vocations, ministries, services, charisms and responsibilities marked by diversity and complementarity. There is only one Holy Spirit who distributes his gifts, charisms and offices and who is "always the dynamic principle of diversity and unity in the Church".[17] As Blessed John Paul II reminded the assembly at the homily of the closing Mass of the 1987 Synod: "What distinguishes persons is *not an increase in dignity,* but *a special and complementary capacity for service.* . . . Thus, the charisms, the ministries, the different forms of service exercised by the lay faithful exist in communion and on behalf of communion. They are treasures that complement one another for the good of all and are under the wise guidance of the

---

[16] *Apostolicam Actuositatem,* 19.
[17] *Christifideles Laici,* 20.

Pastors."[18] Pastors have the role, "not indeed to extinguish the Spirit, but to test all things and hold fast to that which is good (cf. 1 Th. 5:12, 19–21)".[19]

---

[18] Ibid., 20. Emphasis in original.
[19] *Lumen Gentium*, 12.

5

The Specific Role of the Laity

With this chapter we come to the central message of this book. What is the specific role of the laity in the apostolate? What is it that is so distinctive of the lay apostolate that it distinguishes it from the apostolate of the clergy and of the religious? We shall explore this question by studying what the Church teaches us in such documents of the Second Vatican Council as the Pastoral Constitution on the Church in the Modern World *Gaudium et Spes*; the Dogmatic Constitution on the Church *Lumen Gentium*; and the Decree on the Lay Apostolate *Apostolicam Actuositatem*. Pope Paul VI teaches on this subject in his Exhortation after the 1974 Synod on evangelization, *Evangelii Nuntiandi*. Blessed John Paul II does the same in *Christifideles Laici*. Pope Benedict XVI stressed the point on many occasions. And in speaking of the lay faithful, we must not forget the young people. They need special mention.

The message of *Gaudium et Spes*, 43

The teaching of the Second Vatican Council in its Pastoral Constitution on the Church *Gaudium et Spes* is so rich and central to our present topic that it has become the title of this whole book: "Let the layperson take on his own distinctive role." A rather detailed analysis of this famous paragraph will be useful.

The title that the Council gives to the whole paragraph is "The Help Which the Church Strives to Give to Human Activity through Christians". The Council begins by teaching that Christians should synthesize their duties as Christians and their duties as citizens. They should strive to discharge their earthly duties conscientiously and in response to the Gospel spirit. Those Christians are mistaken who, knowing that we have on earth no abiding city but seek one that is to come (Heb 13:14), think that they may therefore shirk their earthly responsibilities. Such people are forgetting that by the faith itself they are more than ever obliged to carry out these duties, each person according to his own vocation.

The Council equally condemns the divorce between religion and daily life. It says that people are mistaken to imagine that religion consists only in acts of worship and the discharge of certain moral obligations and therefore figure they can plunge into earthly affairs as if these were altogether divorced from their faith. In more generalized language, we can call such people the Catholics for whom religion consists in Sunday Mass but for whom whatever they do Monday through Saturday has nothing to do with their Christianity. The Council declares such a mentality to be wrong: "This split between the faith which many profess and their daily lives deserves to be counted among the more serious errors of our age. Long since, the prophets of the Old Testament fought vehemently against this scandal and even more so did Jesus Christ Himself in the New Testament threaten it with grave punishments."

The Council therefore says that there should be no false opposition between professional and social activities, on the one hand, and religious life, on the other. Then it pronounces the following verdict, which is rather severe, considering that it comes from an ecumenical or general council: "The Christian who neglects his temporal duties neglects his duties toward his neighbor and even God, and jeopardizes his eternal salvation." Every layperson, and not just clerics and religious, should take these solemn words to heart. Laypeople are to strive, in the exercise of all their earthly activities, to gather their humane, domestic, professional, social and technical enterprises into one vital synthesis with religious duties, under the supreme direction of which all things are harmonized unto God's glory.

The Council now moves nearer to the heart of the matter: the apostolate that specifically marks out the lay faithful. It says that secular duties and activities belong properly, though not exclusively, to laypeople. As citizens of the world, they are to observe the laws proper to each discipline and labor to equip themselves with competence, each person in his profession. They will learn to cooperate with other citizens and to break new ground in progress in their various fields of engagement.

The Christianization of the temporal order, or the bringing of the spirit of the Gospel into secular affairs, is the apostolate specific to the laity. The Council is clear:

> Laymen should also know that it is generally the function of their well-formed Christian conscience to see that the divine law is inscribed in the life of the earthly city. From priests they may look for spiritual light and nourishment. Let the layman not imagine that his pastors are always such experts, that to every problem which arises, however complicated, they can readily give him a concrete solution, or even that such is their mission. Rather, enlightened by Christian wisdom and giving close attention to the teaching authority of the Church, let the layman take on his own distinctive role.

This is the central message of this book. The apostolate specific to the lay faithful is the animation of the secular sphere of life, that is, family, work, leisure, trade, science, technology, politics, government, international relations and so on. In such matters the laity are to take responsibility on their own. This is where they are particularly called to give witness to Christ. From priests they will receive solid Catholic doctrine and the nourishment of the sacraments. But they are not to expect leadership from the clergy in secular matters. This is not the mission of the clergy. These are areas of their apostolate where the lay faithful should take on their own distinctive role.

The Second Vatican Council is realistic enough to know that there can be differences of opinion among the laity on the best way to animate the secular spheres just mentioned. In seeking to fulfill their mission, differences of views and approaches among the laity are legitimate, depending on the question at hand. In such situations, no layperson or group of laity should try to appropriate the Church's authority. Rather, honest discussion should be promoted, together with mutual charity and respect for the common good.

The Council therefore proposes to the lay faithful an apostolate that is very dynamic and demanding. "Since they have an active role to play in the whole life of the Church, laymen are not only bound to penetrate the world with a Christian spirit. They are also called to be witnesses to Christ in all things in the midst of human society."

In the rest of this paragraph 43, the Council goes on to spell out what it expects from bishops and priests so that the laity can carry out their own specific apostolate and in order that the Church as a whole may give all the help that she is meant to give to human society. We shall consider these points in a later chapter of this book.

The teaching of *Lumen Gentium*, 30–38

The Second Vatican Council issued the Dogmatic Constitution on the Church *Lumen Gentium* in 1964, one year before *Gaudium et Spes*. In paragraphs 30 to 38 of *Lumen Gentium*, the Council states its basic theology of the lay faithful in the Church and discusses as well the apostolate that flows from it and their relations with bishops and priests.

The lay faithful are those who by Baptism are incorporated into Christ and are sent to witness to Christ in the secular sphere. By the will of Christ some men are pastors and teachers in the Church on behalf of others, but all the baptized "share a true equality with regard to the dignity and to the activity common to all the faithful for the building up of the Body of Christ" (no. 32).

The lay apostolate is a participation in the saving mission of the Church herself. All the laity, through their Baptism and Confirmation, are commissioned to that apostolate by the Lord himself. They are nourished especially by the Holy Eucharist.

The Council goes on to state the specific quality of the lay apostolate: "The laity are called in a special way to make the Church present and operative in those places and circumstances where only through them can she become the salt of the earth" (no. 33). Besides this apostolate, there is also the collaboration by the laity with the clergy in what we have described above as inner-Church affairs.

In paragraphs 34 through 36 the Council teaches how the lay faithful, by Baptism, have a share in Christ, who is priest, prophet and king. They share in Christ's priestly functions because "all their works, prayers, and apostolic endeavors, their ordinary married and family life, their daily labor, their mental and physical relaxation, if carried out in the Spirit, and even the hardships of life, if patiently borne —all of these become spiritual sacrifices acceptable to God through Jesus Christ" (no. 34). Christ fulfills his prophetic office "not only through the hierarchy who teach in His name and with His authority, but also through the laity. For that very purpose He made them His witnesses and gave them understanding of the faith and the grace of speech . . . so that the power of the gospel might shine forth in their daily social and family life" (no. 35). The Council appreciates the fact that the laity carry out this prophetic witness in the secular sphere: "The laity go forth as powerful heralds of a faith in things to be hoped for . . . , provided they steadfastly join to their profession of faith a life springing from faith. This evangelization, that is, this announcing of Christ by a living testimony as well as by the spoken word, takes on a specific quality and a special force in that it is carried out in the ordinary surroundings of the world" (no. 35).

Christ as king wishes the laity to spread his kingdom, namely,

> a kingdom of truth and life, a kingdom of holiness and grace, a kingdom of justice, love, and peace. In this kingdom, creation itself will be delivered out of its slavery to corruption and into the freedom of the glory of the sons of God. . . . The faithful, therefore, must learn the deepest meaning and the value of all creation, and how to relate it to the praise of God. They must assist one another to live holier lives even in their daily occupations. In this way the world is permeated by the spirit of Christ and more effectively achieves its purpose in justice, charity, and peace. The laity have the principal role in the universal fulfillment of this purpose. (no. 36)

We can therefore say that the Council sees as specific to the lay apostolate the evangelization of the secular order:

> By their competence in secular fields and by their personal activity, elevated from within by the grace of Christ, let them labor vigorously so that by human labor, technical skill, and civic culture created goods may be perfected for the benefit of every last man, according to the design of the Creator and the light of His Word. Let them work to see that created goods are more fittingly distributed among men, and that such goods in their own way lead to general progress in human and Christian liberty. In this manner, through the members of the Church, Christ will progressively illumine the whole of human society with His saving light. (no. 36)

Thus the laity are to persevere in promoting cultural values, in harmonizing faith and civic duties and in guaranteeing religious freedom for citizens.

In paragraphs 37 and 38, the Council urges dialogue between the laity and their pastors, a strengthened sense of personal responsibility in the laity, respect by the pastors of this just freedom of the laity and ready cooperation by laypersons in the projects of their pastors. The Council also stresses how necessary it is for each individual layperson to stand before the world as a witness to the Resurrection and life of the Lord Jesus and as a sign that God lives.

All this is very encouraging. The lay faithful are furnished with the theology that defines their life in Christ and the Church and the consequent apostolate expected of them in the Church and in the world. *Gaudium et Spes* and *Apostolicam Actuositatem* were issued a year after *Lumen Gentium* in order to go into greater detail on this apostolate.

Apostolicam Actuositatem on the
specificity of the lay apostolate

We focus at this point on what the Fathers of the Second Vatican Council in their Decree on the Lay Apostolate, *Apostolicam Actuositatem*, say about what is most specific to the apostolate of the lay faithful. Paragraphs 5 to 8 deal with the matter.

The Council reminds us that Christ's redemptive work, while of itself directed toward the salvation of people, involves also the renewal of the whole temporal order. That is why the mission of the Church is not only to bring people the message and grace of Christ but also to penetrate and perfect the temporal sphere with the spirit of the Gospel. It is in fulfilling this mission of the Church that the lay faithful exercise their apostolate both in the Church and in the world, in both the spiritual and temporal orders. Christ wants to make the whole universe into a new creation (no. 5).

The mission of the Church concerns the salvation of people, which is to be achieved by belief in Christ and by his grace. The Church strives to manifest Christ's message by words and deeds and to communicate his grace to the world. The clergy do this work through the ministry of the word and the administration of the sacraments. The laity have an important role to play because they are "fellow workers in the truth" (3 Jn 8). They do this not only by the example of their good lives and the words they address directly to believers and nonbelievers, but more particularly by what they do to face the problems of the world of today according to Christian principles (no. 6).

In paragraph 7 the Council comes to the core of its statement concerning the distinctiveness of the lay apostolate. God's plan for the world is that people should work together to restore the temporal sphere of things and to develop it unceasingly. By "temporal sphere" is meant family, culture, economic affairs, the arts and professions, political institutions and international relations, as well as their development and progress. These elements not only help the attainment of mankind's ultimate goal but also possess their own intrinsic value. Sin, however, the Council notes, is a sad fact in human history, original sin and actual sin. Sin has corrupted morals and human institutions, damaged human beings and made some people slaves of science and technology instead of their masters. The whole Church must work hard to help mankind to direct the temporal order to God through Christ. Pastors do this by teaching the correct doctrine on the purpose and use of temporal things and making available the moral and spiritual aids by which the temporal order can be restored in Christ. But this is the area where the lay faithful in particular are called to operate. The incisive words of the Council are worth quoting in full because they restate in a different way the main burden of this book.

> The laity must take on the renewal of the temporal order as their own special obligation. Led by the light of the gospel and the mind of the Church, and motivated by Christian love, let them act directly and definitively in the temporal sphere. As citizens they must cooperate with other citizens, using their own particular skills and acting on their own responsibility. Everywhere and in all things they must seek the justice characteristic of God's kingdom. The temporal order must be renewed in such a way that, without the slightest detriment to its own proper laws, it can be brought into conformity with the higher principles of the Christian life

and adapted to the shifting circumstances of time, place, and person. Outstanding among the works of this type of apostolate is that of Christian social action. This sacred Synod desires to see it extended now to the whole temporal sphere, including culture. (no. 7)

In paragraph 8 the Council speaks of the importance of works of charity and projects of social assistance and insists that the lay faithful should be actively involved in their promotion.

One can see from the above quotations that the Council Fathers continue in this Decree on the Lay Apostolate to emphasize that what is specific to the lay faithful is witnessing to Christ in the spheres that make up the temporal order. This is their distinctive role.

Pope Paul VI in *Evangelii Nuntiandi*

In 1974 the Third General Assembly of the Synod of Bishops had evangelization as its theme. On December 8, 1975, Pope Paul VI issued his Apostolic Exhortation *Evangelii Nuntiandi*. Among the workers for evangelization, he discusses the laity and their role in paragraph 70.

The pope sets the scene by stating that laypeople, because their vocation places them in the midst of the world and in charge of the most varied temporal tasks, must for this very reason exercise a very special form of evangelization. "Their primary and immediate task is not to establish and develop the ecclesial community—this is the specific role of the pastors—but to put to use every Christian and evangelical possibility latent but already present and active in the affairs of the world." Pope Paul then goes on to spell out in some detail the areas where the lay faithful should be particularly active:

> Their own field of evangelizing activity is the vast and complicated world of politics, society and economics, but also the world of culture, of the sciences and the arts, of international life, of the mass media. It also includes other realities which are open to evangelization, such as human love, the family, the education of children and adolescents, professional work, suffering. The more Gospel-inspired lay people there are engaged in these realities, clearly involved in them, competent to promote them and conscious that they must exercise to the full their Christian powers which are often buried and suffocated, the more these realities will be at the service of the Kingdom of God and therefore of salvation in Jesus Christ, without in any way losing or sacrificing their human content but rather pointing to a transcendent dimension which is often disregarded.[1]

This papal teaching is perfectly in line with what the Second Vatican Council declared.

Blessed John Paul II in *Christifideles Laici*

Blessed John Paul II, among other elements, stresses the secular character of the call of the lay faithful to the apostolate, particularly in paragraph 15 of his Post-synodal Apostolic Exhortation *Christifideles Laici*. The newness of the Christian life is the foundation and title for equality among all the baptized in Christ. Because of the one dignity flowing from Baptism, each member of the lay faithful, together with ordained ministers and men and women religious, shares a responsibility for the Church's mission. A secular character

---

[1] Paul VI, Apostolic Exhortation *Evangelii Nuntiandi*, 70.

is properly and particularly that of the lay faithful. The Church lives in the world, even if she is not of the world (cf. Jn 17:16). She is sent to continue the redemptive work of Jesus Christ, which concerns the salvation of mankind and also involves the renewal of the whole temporal order.

The laypeople receive their call to the Christian life from God in the secular world. They "live in the world, that is, in every one of the secular professions and occupations. They live in the ordinary circumstances of family and social life, from which the very fabric of their existence is woven."[2] This condition of the lay faithful is not simply an external and environmental framework but a reality *destined to find in Jesus Christ the fullness of its meaning*. Blessed John Paul then quotes the Second Vatican Council, which says that "the Word made flesh willed to share in human fellowship. . . . He sanctified those human ties, especially family ones, from which social relationships arise, willingly submitting himself to the laws of his country. He chose to lead the life of an ordinary craftsman of his own time and place."[3]

Blessed John Paul II is now in a position to make his central statement in this paragraph, namely, that the world, the secular sphere, is the place where the lay faithful are called to live their Christian life. They do not just happen to find themselves there. That is where God calls them as Christians to give witness to Christ as members of the Church. The pope says: "The 'world' thus becomes the place and the means for the lay faithful to fulfill their Christian vocation, because the world itself is destined to glorify God the Father in Christ. . . . The lay faithful, in fact, 'are called by God so that they, led by the spirit of the Gospel, might contribute to the sanctification of the world, as from within

---

[2] *Christifideles Laici*, 15, quoting *Lumen Gentium*, 31.
[3] Ibid., quoting *Gaudium et Spes*, 32.

like leaven, by fulfilling their own particular duties. Thus, especially in their way of life, resplendent in faith, hope and charity they manifest Christ to others.'"[4] The pope therefore states the following memorable words: "Thus for the lay faithful, to be present and active in the world is not only an anthropological and sociological reality, but in a specific way, a theological and ecclesiological reality as well. In fact, in their situation in the world God manifests his plan and communicates to them their particular vocation of 'seeking the Kingdom of God by engaging in temporal affairs and by ordering them according to the plan of God'."[5]

Blessed John Paul II consequently says that the lay faithful's position in the Church is fundamentally defined by their *newness in Christian life* and distinguished by their *secular character*. He observes that the Gospel images of salt, light and leaven, although indiscriminately applicable to all Jesus' disciples, are specifically applied to the lay faithful. These are particularly meaningful images because they not only speak of the deep involvement and the full participation of the lay faithful in the affairs of the earth, the world and the human community but also and above all tell of the radical newness and unique character of an involvement and a participation that has as its purpose the spreading of the Gospel that brings salvation.

All this goes to show that Catholics are mistaken if they imagine that the most active lay apostles in the parish are those laypeople who read the Scriptures at Mass or help the priest to distribute Holy Communion. Of course, Church law in the Latin Rite sometimes permits extraordinary ministers of Holy Communion when the ordinary ministers are not sufficient to handle the number of communicants

---

[4] Ibid., quoting *Lumen Gentium*, 31.
[5] Ibid.

and when the diocesan arrangement allows it. And laymen and laywomen may read the Scriptures, although not the Gospels, at Mass even if they are not installed lectors. But these are not examples of the lay faithful acting at the height of their mission. It is rather when the laity are active in bringing the plan and law of God into every level of the government, the trade unions, the family, the medical profession, the university, the media and so on. These are examples of the secular spheres where laypeople are theologically, and as members of the Church, called to exercise their apostolate. These are sectors of life where the laity are called to take on their own distinctive role.

Pope Benedict XVI

Let us select four passages from the many teachings of Pope Benedict XVI on the same doctrine.

In his first Encyclical Letter, *Deus Caritas Est*, the pope discussed the working out of justice and charity in society. He says that the formation of just structures is not directly the duty of the Church but belongs to the world of politics. But the Church has an indirect duty here because she has to contribute to the purification of reason and the reawakening of moral forces. The pope then spoke directly of the role of the laity:

> The direct duty to work for a just ordering of society, on the other hand, is proper to the lay faithful. As citizens of the State, they are called to take part in public life in a personal capacity. So they cannot relinquish their participation "in the many different economic, social, legislative, administrative and cultural areas, which are intended to promote organically and institutionally the *common good*". The mission of the lay faithful is therefore to configure social life cor-

rectly, respecting its legitimate autonomy and cooperating with other citizens according to their respective competencies and fulfilling their own responsibility.[6]

In his address to the Ecclesial Convention of the Diocese of Rome on May 26, 2009, the pope said that the lay faithful should not be seen as just collaborators with the clergy but rather as "co-responsible", because every member of the Church shares responsibility for the mission of the Church: "This demands a change in mindset, particularly concerning lay people. They must no longer be viewed as 'collaborators' of the clergy but truly recognized as 'co-responsible', for the Church's being and action, thereby fostering the consolidation of a mature and committed laity. This common awareness of being Church of all the baptized in no way diminishes the responsibility of parish priests."[7]

In his address to the Plenary Assembly of the Pontifical Council for the Laity on November 25, 2011, speaking on the importance of reawakening the question of God in modern society, he dwelt on the role of the laity:

> The question about God is revealed by the encounter with those who have the gift of faith, with those who have a vital relationship with the Lord. God comes to be known through men and women who know him: the path towards him passes concretely through those who have met him. Your role as faithful lay people is particularly important here. . . . You are called to bear a transparent witness to the importance of the question of God in every field of thought and action.[8]

Speaking to some US bishops on radical secularism—which finds increasing expression in the political and cultural spheres—during their *ad limina* visit to him on January

---

[6] *Deus Caritas Est*, 29, quoting *Christifideles Laici*, 42.

[7] *L'Osservatore Romano*, weekly English ed., June 3, 2009, p. 4.

[8] Ibid., December 14, 2011, p. 14.

19, 2012, Pope Benedict again stressed the importance of the role of the laity:

> Here once more we see the need for an engaged, articulate and well-formed Catholic laity endowed with a strong critical sense vis-à-vis the dominant culture and with the courage to counter a reductive secularism which would delegitimize the Church's participation in public debate about the issues which are determining the future of American society. The preparation of committed lay leaders and the presentation of a convincing articulation of the Christian vision of man and society remain a primary task of the Church in your country; as essential components of the new evangelization, these concerns must shape the vision and goals of catechetical programs at every level. In this regard, I would mention with appreciation your efforts to maintain contacts with Catholics involved in political life and to help them understand their personal responsibility to offer public witness to their faith, especially with regard to the great moral issues of our time: respect for God's gift of life, the protection of human dignity and the promotion of authentic human rights. . . . There can be no doubt that a more consistent witness on the part of America's Catholics to their deepest convictions would make a major contribution to the renewal of society as a whole.[9]

From these samples of the teachings of Pope Benedict XVI, it is clear that the Holy Father repeats the teaching of the importance of lay witness in the secular sphere and applies it to varying situations.

The young not forgotten

References to the laity in this book should not be restricted to adult laypeople. The young lay faithful are included, ex-

[9] Ibid., January 25, 2012, p. 3.

cept where the context implies otherwise. The young must not be forgotten. Space has to be made for them.

In African countries, in Asia, especially India, and in Latin America, young people make up a majority of the population. Their youthfulness is a gift and a treasure from God for which the whole Church is grateful to the Lord of life. Young people should be loved, esteemed and respected.[10] It is estimated that Blessed John Paul II addressed between twenty and twenty-five million young people in the World Youth Day rallies alone.

Youth is a time when genuine and irrepressible questions arise about the meaning of life and the direction our lives should take.[11] The Rule of Saint Benedict directs the abbot of the monastery to listen to the youngest monks first because it is often to a younger brother that the Lord reveals the best course. Thus, says Pope Benedict XVI, "we should make every effort to involve young people directly in the life of society and of the Church, so that they do not fall prey to feelings of frustration and rejection in the face of their inability to shape their own future."[12]

This advice should be borne in mind not only in the organization of movements and associations for young people but also in larger parish and lay apostolate associations and organizations. Sometimes a young person can inspire hope and initiative where his elders consider that not much can be done.

Young people should not only ask what is to be done for them. They should also ask themselves what contribution they can make to society as young people. Their apostolate can begin with their peer groups. If they are students, how

---

[10] Cf. *Africae Munus*, 60.

[11] Cf. Benedict XVI, Post-synodal Apostolic Exhortation *Verbum Domini*, 104; *Africae Munus*, 61.

[12] *Africae Munus*, 62.

are they meeting the challenges posed to Christian students in matters touching on honesty in examinations, respect for their parents, nobility in boy-girl relationships and care of school property? If they are young workers, what are they doing among their colleagues to improve relationships between employers and employees? How are they making their work a real manifestation of solidarity with other people, especially by being honest and efficient? What are young people doing to improve the attitude of their peers toward their civic duties, by way of respect for the law and involvement in politics and government? How are they helping their peers to grow into a mature understanding about the responsibilities involved in starting families of their own?

Whether, therefore, the layperson is an elder member of society, a young person or someone in between, the central message is that laypeople must take on their own distinctive role in society.

6

Some Reasons for the Urgent Need of the Lay Apostolate

Reasons for the urgent need of the lay apostolate have been included in many of the foregoing reflections. But now it is useful to spell out some of these reasons in a more formal way.

Where God is left out of life in society

The phenomenon of God being left out of life in society is growing in one country after another in the world of today. Of course in countries where an atheistic or communist ideology holds sway, there is not only a deliberate effort to exclude God from life, but there is even positive aggressiveness toward the idea of the existence of God. Fortunately, such countries are a minority in the world today.

What obtains more often, even in some countries that have been traditionally Christian, is that some currents in society make less and less room for God. They do not even take the trouble to deny the existence of God. They simply live, and want others to live, as if God did not exist. This secularism appears in their families, in their schools, in places of work and recreation, in the mass media, in politics and government and in the promotion of science and technology. It can be called practical atheism. This ideology is also brought into the running of international organizations, including those for social services and for help to refugees and displaced people.

The pope and the bishops are expected to propagate the truth about God as Creator, Providence and Judge of all mankind and as the origin of human society, the Maker whose instructions society has to follow if, indeed, society does not want to end in a fiasco. And priests preach the same saving truth.

Nevertheless, it is the lay faithful who live in the secular sphere, who meet their colleagues in the various arenas mentioned above, and who are better placed not only to witness by word but also, and especially, to show by the example of their lives that human society has to pay attention to God. Indeed, the personal example of a layperson in how to live in society today can convince more than the example set by a cleric or a religious, because people presume that these latter live in a more protected enclosure, whereas a layperson is "one of themselves".

Pope Benedict XVI, speaking to the Plenary Assembly of the Pontifical Council for the Laity on November 25, 2011, stressed the importance of the personal example of the laity in drawing people to God:

> The question about God is revealed by the encounter with those who have the gift of faith, with those who have a vital relationship with the Lord. God comes to be known through men and women who know him: the path towards him passes concretely through those who have met him. Your role as faithful lay people is particularly important here.
>
> As *Christifideles Laici* notes, this is your specific vocation: in the Church's mission "a particular place falls to the lay faithful by reason of their 'secular character', obliging them, in their proper and irreplaceable way, to work towards the Christian animation of the temporal order" (no. 36). You

are called to bear a transparent witness to the importance of the question of God in every field of thought and action. In the family, at work, as well as in politics and in the economy, people of today need to see for themselves and to feel tangibly how with God, or without God, everything changes.[1]

If secularism, or the attempt to elbow God out of private and public life, is to be fought to a finish, then the active involvement of convinced laypeople is indispensable. Pope Benedict XVI often dwelt on the importance of new evangelization, particularly in those areas that have been traditionally Christian but are now losing something of their original Christian vitality. He has even instituted a new office or dicastery among the central offices of the Church to promote this apostolate. The laity have an important role to play in the new evangelization.

Contemporary culture and faith

Faith and culture have to meet. By their active involvement in society, Christians are able to influence their culture in a better, more authentic and more incisive way.

By the Incarnation, the Son of God took on human nature and inserted himself into a concrete and particular culture, people, language, forms of expression and rituals of celebration.

The Christian has to learn from the Incarnation to be a legitimate and authentic child of his time, his people, his society, his country. The Gospel has the power to give life to a culture.

[1] Papal address on November 25, 2011, in *L'Osservatore Romano,* weekly English ed., December 14, 2011, p. 11.

> Since the kingdom of Christ is not of this world (cf. Jn.
> 18:36), the Church or People of God takes nothing away
> from the temporal welfare of any people by establishing that
> kingdom. Rather does she foster and take to herself, insofar
> as they are good, the ability, resources, and customs of each
> people. Taking them to herself she purifies, strengthens, and
> ennobles them. The Church in this is mindful that she must
> harvest with that King to whom the nations were given for
> an inheritance (Ps. 2:8) and into whose city they bring gifts
> and presents (cf. Ps. 71[72]:10; Is. 60:4–7; Apoc. 21:24).[2]

The Christian should be a credible witness of this truth.
He should work to make the culture one in which he can
comfortably live and express his faith. And the person best
placed to do this is not the cleric or the religious but the
layperson.

It is for the laity, each according to his profession and competence, to show positively in society, and to argue when
necessary, that encounter with the Gospel of Jesus all along
the corridors of two millennia has been an event of inspira-
tion and elevation for cultures and has built bridges between
peoples. Moreover, it has enriched the fiber of social relations, inspired the arts, humanized and elevated education
and been a powerful motivation for works of charity and
mercy.

Here special mention can be made regarding the important role that the lay faithful have in colleges and universities. Even in Catholic universities and colleges, the academic community is generally composed largely of laypeople.
These lay Catholics should respond in a significant way to
the call of the Church "to be present, as signs of courage
and intellectual creativity, in the privileged areas of culture,
that is, the world of education—school and university—

---

[2] *Lumen Gentium*, 13.

in places of scientific and technological research, the areas of artistic creativity and work in the humanities."[3] "The Church sees their developing presence in these institutions both as a sign of hope and as a confirmation of the irreplaceable lay vocation in the Church and in the world."[4]

In defense of marriage and the family

Marriage and the family are fundamental institutions in every society, culture and nation. Their well-being or the lack of it affects all in society. If these two institutions are in a healthy state, there is hope for that society, culture and nation.

There are, however, some forces that militate against marriage and the family by banalizing, desacralizing, commercializing or ridiculing them. It is enough to think of ideologies that glamorize sexual relations outside marriage, that give marital infidelity the apparently innocuous name of affairs and that regard divorce as an obvious right. There are anti-life forces that regard children as a burden and that consider contraception and abortion as fundamental health care rights of every woman. There are people who regard euthanasia as a right that a doctor should help a sick person to exercise. As for homosexuality and same-sex unions, do most people really need arguments to see that these are not according to the Maker's instructions?

Many societies make it ever more difficult for the parents to exercise their right as the primary educators of their children. In some countries it is difficult to find schools

---

[3] *Christifideles Laici,* 44.
[4] John Paul II, Apostolic Constitution on Catholic Universities *Ex Corde Ecclesiae,* 25.

that share the religious convictions of the parents and that can therefore safely educate the children without sabotaging what the parents are striving to do at home. This has at times compelled some parents to undertake homeschooling, with all that this implies. There are many countries where religion is forbidden in the public schools or where programs of so-called sex education offend against what the parents hold sacred.

The Second Vatican Council issued a Decree on Christian Education. Practically every pope in our times has written and spoken about the proper education of children. Bishops have done the same thing in various ways. And priests are active on the matter, too. But none of this action by clerics can replace the witness needed from the lay faithful. The children who go to school are theirs. It is the laypeople who are members of parliaments where the laws are made. They should rise up and be counted!

As to the defense of marriage and the family, it is obvious that the layperson's witness in the mass media, in parliaments, in governments, and in academic institutions is irreplaceable. Laypeople will find much solid information in the 525-page document: *Compendium of the Social Doctrine of the Church*. If candidates seeking political election are pro-abortion or if they support the dissemination of RU-486 and the so-called morning-after pill or if they want euthanasia legalized, should well-informed laypeople not spring into action to defend life and the family?

It will be very helpful to the laity in their defense of marriage and the family to study carefully the Post-synodal Apostolic Exhortation *Familiaris Consortio*. This major document was issued by Blessed John Paul II in 1981 after the 1980 Synod of Bishops on the role of the Christian family in the world of today. The Second Vatican Council had already called the family "the domestic church",[5] a "community of love".[6] The intimate partnership of married life and love, says the Council, "is rooted in the conjugal covenant of irrevocable personal consent".[7] "The family is a kind of school of deeper humanity."[8] "The future of humanity", says *Familiaris Consortio*, "passes by way of the family. It is therefore indispensable and urgent that every person of good will should endeavor to save and foster the values and requirements of the family."[9] Laypeople should regard the defense of marriage and the family as an apostolate to which they are particularly called. Their good example as model husbands and wives and their promotion of family prayer and of harmony and reconciliation between the family members are an excellent witness.

Single men and women who are singles also have an important witness to give in the Church and in the world. This witness differs from that of married people and of priests and religious. Single people can give witness to Christian lives marked by generosity, attention to the poor, the orphan and the handicapped, involvement in various Church works and a general sense of peace and joy and readiness to engage in voluntary apostolates.

Urbanization and population movements

In most countries in the world there is a marked influx of people from rural areas to big cities, particularly by the

---

[5] *Lumen Gentium*, 11; *Christifideles Laici*, 47, 62.
[6] *Gaudium et Spes*, 47.
[7] Ibid., 48.
[8] Ibid., 52.
[9] John Paul II, Apostolic Exhortation *Familiaris Consortio*, 86.

younger generation. In cities there are often such phenom-
ena as unemployment, unsuitable living conditions, conges-
tion and air pollution, especially at the peripheries of cities.
From the relatively quiet life in the village where everybody knew everybody else, the new arrival in the city is
forced into anonymity, an individual struggle for survival
and an undeclared rush of "everybody for himself and the
devil take the last". At the same time, the city dweller is
bombarded by television programs and advertisements that
portray life as easy, sweet, comfortable and pleasant. Many
advertisements strive to sell him unnecessary creature com-
forts as real needs. To make things worse, the new city arrival sees a few people who are provocatively rich and who
spend money with reckless abandon. He is gradually being
fed a materialistic culture. Is it any surprise if such an unemployed young person who is hungry and angry is approached
for recruitment by a ill-defined group that proposes instant
comfort and riches, even if at times violence is required?

Unrestrained city population growth has generated, indeed precipitated, problems that challenge even parishes run
by very capable priests. "The harvest is plentiful, but the laborers are few" (Mt 9:37). "The children beg for food, but
no one gives to them" (Lam 4:4). People are hungry for
Christ, especially in the big cities and suburbs. The challenges are so immense that the clergy cannot cope singlehandedly. Laypeople are needed to help share with these
populations hope, fraternity, gratuitousness, kindness and
Christian solidarity. They are also needed to find solutions
to unemployment and poor housing and to provide soup
kitchens, help to young people seeking suitable conditions
for apprenticeship, laws regarding remuneration for house
servants and protection against child labor, not to speak
of human trafficking. Even the poor unemployed and the

homeless can ask themselves what they can do in the apostolate among those who share with them the same precarious situations of life. One does not need to be a member of a powerful organization in order to witness to Christ among the poorest of the poor.

The Catholic movement, Community of Sant'Egidio, is known for its nearness to deprived people and its help in reconciling warring groups. Pope Benedict XVI encouraged the members in his address to them in the Basilica of Saint Bartholomew on Tiber Island in Rome on April 7, 2008:

> As children of this Church which presides in charity, you then spread your charism to many other parts of the world. The Word of God, love for the Church, special love for the poor and the communication of the Gospel have been the stars that guided you while you witnessed, under different skies, to the one message of Christ. I thank you for your apostolic work; I thank you for your attention to the least and for your quest for peace, which is a characteristic of your Community. . . . Be true friends of God and authentic friends of humanity. And do not fear the difficulties and suffering that this missionary action entails.[10]

Earlier the basic ecclesial communities were mentioned as particularly active, for example, in many countries in East Africa. They also know how to be near people who have to struggle with the challenges posed by urbanization and population movements. They help settle family and community quarrels. They assist the ordinary Christian to live the faith in the harsh realities of daily life such as the poor often know it.

---

[10] Quoted by Andrea Riccardi, in Pontifical Council for the Laity, *Pastors and the Ecclesial Movements* (Rome: Libreria Editrice Vaticana, 2009), pp. 192–93.

Mass media and cultural thought patterns

The Church in every country can ask herself what image of the Gospel is present in the mass media and in cultural thought patterns in the country in question. In some countries Catholics may be in the majority or at least represent a sizeable percentage of the population. How much are they contributing to the cultural patterns of their society? Are they influential in academia, in the mass media and, in general, in the formation of public opinion? What about playwriting, theatre productions, and amateur films? Are lay Catholics hesitant, slow or even afraid to show their faith in public? Do they hide their faith while religious indifferentists and practical materialists openly and boldly dictate the tune? Are the lay faithful expecting clerics to present the image and message of the Church, while they themselves are satisfied with attending Sunday Mass and receiving Holy Communion? What are the laity contributing to the fabric of society so that life in society will be as near as possible to the Gospel ideal? Do laypeople do nothing when they notice that the mass media present Catholic positions on marriage, the family, defense of unborn life and the importance of religion in education as old-fashioned and conservative?

Evangelization of politics and government

To speak of the evangelization of politics and government can sound a little unnecessarily provocative. And yet it is only reasonable. As we discussed earlier, the specific mission of the lay faithful is to bring the spirit of Christ into the various spheres of the secular order. And politics and government are very much a part of them. They are con-

cerned with the conduct of life in the earthly city. It is God
who gave human beings a social nature. Society is from God.
The manner in which life is conducted in society, therefore,
must accord with the Maker's instructions. This is another
way of saying that politics and government should respect
God's plan, should obey the natural law. They should be
evangelized. And this apostolate is specifically that of the
lay faithful.

It is, therefore, not correct for the laity to shy away from
political involvement. If in a particular country, for instance,
a political party demands that all its candidates for election,
its flag-bearers, should be in favor of abortion, that party is
violating freedom of conscience. In other words, that party
is not allowing its members the freedom to follow what
they are convinced is God's natural law. People should take
action to get that political party to change its policy. This
is an ideal apostolate for the laity.

If a political party or a government discriminates against
people because of their religious affiliation, it should not be
allowed to get away with such repression of the human person. The defense of fundamental human rights, such as the
right to religious freedom and practice, calls for the active
involvement of the lay faithful.

If the laws of a country discriminate against families with
several children and in practice make it very difficult for a
worker with an average salary to rent a flat and educate his
children, then courageous, farsighted laypeople are needed
who will not hesitate to come to the public forum to defend
the fundamental cell of society that is the family.

The presentation of the Christian position on social questions, when made by laypeople who are well prepared, has
a special power to convince the general public. Newspaper articles, television programs, parliamentary debates and
well-informed books are some of the ways in which to

give such witness. Website designers, computer programmers and electronic apps creators also have their importance. Laypeople could also buy airtime for the broadcasting of religious programs. Personal example always has its power to persuade. Very symbolic and convincing is the example of that king who resigned his kingship rather than sign a law in favor of abortion. Such action is worth more than a thousand words. Constant vigilance is needed on the part of the laity to see that the laws that govern society always respect the divine plan for mankind, the natural law that guides human action.

Witness to honest living

In many countries, corruption is becoming widespread in fields like high finance, politics, civil service, trade and commerce and even sports. This is a big challenge to harmonious living, mutual trust and steady economic development. Christians cannot remain indifferent in front of this virus. And it is the lay faithful who are in the front line to give witness to honest living. They can achieve much individually and in organized groups.

The menace of violence

In quite a number of nations there is considerable lack of harmony in society; there is tension; and in some cases there is open violence. No one who listens to world news over the radio or the television will fail to note this.

Laypeople have to ask themselves what they can do in order to promote dialogue between citizens, between people of differing religions and between social groups. Acknowledgment of wrongs done to others, forgiveness of injuries and the willingness to reconcile are required for justice and peace. Jesus our Master pronounced blessed those who are peacemakers, for they shall be called children of God (cf. Mt 5:9).

Public face of the Church

Everyone knows that the leaders of the Church are the pope and the bishops in union with him. They are the pastors according to the will of Christ himself. They have priests as their closest collaborators in the pastoral ministry. That is not under discussion or debate.

It is equally true that the Church is the new family of God of which Christ is the Head. The Church is the union of all the baptized in Christ. Membership is by Baptism, which gives to all the followers of Christ a fundamental equality as his disciples. It is this same sacrament which is the foundation of the universal call to every member of the Church to take part in the mission of the Church. It is, therefore, clear that the Church is not identified with clerics. Care has to be taken in the public square to present the Church, not as the society or club of the clerics, but as the communion of all the baptized in Christ.

In many countries, for example, when radio and television want a person to represent the Catholic Church in a debate on such topics as abortion, extramarital relations or euthanasia, they invite a bishop or a priest, but not a Catholic layperson. One may respond that a cleric may be better qualified to state the Catholic position. But could it not be argued that it would be more suitable to base the choice solely on the capacity of the person to state the Catholic belief, whether that person be a cleric, a layperson or a religious? And would it not show better the reality of who is the Church if there were variation in the choice of Catholic exponents? If the choice is always made from among the clerics, is this not a tacit way of saying that the clerics are the Church? And if it is always a cleric who states publicly an unpopular Catholic position, is this not a subtle way of presenting to the public an image of the Church as equivalent to the clergy and also as an institution that is predominantly negative and pessimistic?

Both clerics and laity should not allow such a situation to develop or to continue. It is not a good argument to say that the clergy are better prepared theologically than the laity. Laypeople can also be theologically well prepared. Some lay faithful teach theology in its various branches in seminaries and Catholic colleges and universities. Moreover, witness given by a layperson in matters touching the secular sphere, as has often been insisted in this discussion, has greater convincing power than similar arguments made by a cleric or a religious. And there are arenas where the clerics are not called to function, such as parliaments. Let the laypeople take on their own distinctive role in such matters, and let all clerics, lay faithful and religious be convinced that the Church is all three and that all three should participate in presenting the complete image of the Church.

7

What Some Lay Initiatives Have Achieved

It is now time to mention, no matter how briefly, what lay initiatives have, *de facto*, achieved in some countries. For several reasons, I shall not mention the names of the countries in question.

In one country the national parliament was discussing a bill to introduce a law to liberalize the practice of abortion, that is, to make it easier to kill unborn babies. The Catholic Women's Organization met with the Muslim Women's Organization to adopt a common approach to the major political parties. The National Laity Council also got into action. Clerics furnished some members of parliament with the natural law arguments in defense of unborn life and in illustration of the horrors of abortion. These convinced laypeople worked hard, and, in the end, the national parliament finally rejected the proposal to facilitate the killing of unborn babies.

In another place the government wanted to monopolize the educational system and seized the Church's schools. The bishops protested, made declarations and wrote good pastoral letters, but that did not do the trick. Finally, it was the Catholic women through their organizations that pressurized the political parties and warned the government not to expect their votes at the next elections if the schools were not returned to their rightful owners. This is the type of language that every politician understands. It is not the usual style of bishops' statements. It worked. Some schools were returned to the Church. And the situation continued to improve in the future.

Where Catholics are a small minority of the population or where they are under some form of persecution or discrimination, it is likely that the importance of the lay apostolate is better appreciated. In such situations there are sectors of life where clerics are not welcome and where only the laity can witness to Christ and represent or protect Catholic or Christian interests. During times of persecution, it is easier for the forces against the Church to identify clerics, marginalize them and punish them. It is harder to do that to the lay faithful. In such circumstances, many laypeople have given wonderful and courageous witness to Christ and his Church.

Catholic students who attend public schools where prayers and religious education are not allowed or, worse still, where Christianity is in a subtle way discriminated against have sometimes been found to be more courageous in witnessing to their Catholic faith than Catholic students who attended Catholic schools. The latter have often not learned to organize and fight for their religious rights because they have not experienced the necessity to do so. The argument is not that Catholics should be discriminated against so that they will learn to organize themselves. Rather, it is to say that, de facto, discrimination and marginalization have spurred laypeople on to a greater and more courageous apostolate.

In some countries such as the United States and Indonesia, some laypeople, in an effort to make a positive contribution in the provision of authentic Catholic education, have joined hands and set up colleges and even universities. They have been careful to obtain the required consent and approval from the competent ecclesiastical authority, so that these institutions will rightly have the name Catholic.[1] Such colleges or universities set up by the laity have been greatly trusted and supported by Catholic parents because the parents see that these institutions are unambiguously Catholic and have not succumbed to compromises with a secular culture.

Some lay apostolate organizations have given great attention to the poor, the deprived and the homeless. They organize for the needy, not just a symbolic Christmas lunch, but a hot meal every day for those who have suffered so much that they are not ashamed to benefit from the offer. There is also the practice of making overnight accommodation available to those who are stranded.

Some conflict situations do not easily yield to intervention by large organizations, like the United Nations Organization, or to pressure from rich countries or groups of them. And yet where a particular lay apostolate association makes quiet and prudent contacts, there has sometimes been success. Thus reconciliation was achieved between the government of Mozambique and a breakaway group with which it had been at war for many years. Both sides were persuaded to sit around a discussion table. War weapons were finally silenced. Eventually the Catholic lay association involved, the Community of Sant'Egidio, decided that it had done its job and that it must now leave the rest to the political bodies and the people inside and outside the country. People can speculate about how such an achievement was possible. Motivations based on the Catholic faith shared between the participants, wisdom and experience, respect and Christian love go a long way. But certainly it was neither trade nor

---

[1] Cf. *Ex Corde Ecclesiae*, art 3, §3.

commerce, it was neither oil nor gas, and it was neither international pressure nor election hopes that made the cessation of hostilities possible. It was an example of what lay conviction and consequent engagement can achieve.

Ecumenism is about initiatives and prayers by Catholics, Orthodox, Anglicans and other Ecclesial Communities for the reunion of Christians. No doubt, the leaders of these religious families meet from time to time. But it has also happened that a lay movement, like the Focolare Movement, has been successful in making contacts between leaders of separated Christians or their representatives less difficult. Whoever can promote mutual understanding and harmony should be encouraged.

The thread running through all the above examples is the willingness of laypeople to take action to improve an existing situation. They allow their faith to motivate them to take initiatives indicated by the challenge in front of them. They manifest their faith. The bearers of the paralytic in the Gospel did not allow physical obstacles to prevent them from bringing the sick person in front of Jesus for healing. Without intending to see a parallel in every detail of this Gospel account, we can admire the faith and initiative of these bearers of the sick. And Jesus rewarded their faith. Situations appeal to the laity to show faith and courage and not to hesitate to assume their own distinctive role.

8

Reasons for Hesitation
regarding Lay Engagement

Some may think that having the laity take the initiative and responsibility to evangelize the secular sphere looks like an attractive and dynamic doctrine but feel there are legitimate reasons for hesitation. They are afraid of what might happen. They consider the risk to be too great. They prefer the beaten track where the clergy give the needed leadership and all goes well. They say that this has served the Church and society well for centuries and that there is no need to venture into uncharted waters. These are serious reasons that need to be addressed at this point.

The clergy give good leadership:
there is no need to change

In many countries where there is a Catholic majority in the population, it has been the custom for the clergy to give most of the leadership, not only in inner-Church affairs but also in socio-cultural and sometimes even in political matters. They have generally been among the most learned people around. They have seen what needed to be done. They have given orders. The laity have trusted them and obeyed them. They have looked after the spiritual welfare of the population. They have also taken care of their material well-being. An extreme situation was reached when some bishops became local princes with secular concerns for their people, and the pope himself, through governors, ruled some parts of what is now Italy as Papal States. This situation no longer exists and is now not regarded as desirable, even if much good was done through it, especially during the period of the Vandal invasions of Rome.

As a result of all this, is that some clerics began to identify the Church with the clergy and to regard the mission of the Church as coextensive with the apostolate of the clergy. When some priests, and even some bishops, said "the Church", they meant the bishops and the priests. The lay apostolate was unwittingly regarded as a help to the clerics or as a participation in the apostolate of the bishops or as the long arm of the clergy.

It is understandable that, in such situations, structures in the Church that foresee a specific apostolate for the laity will be long in coming. Thus parish councils with elected members, diocesan financial councils and laity councils with elected leaders at parish, diocesan and national levels may not be well received by all. And the reason is that both the clerics and the lay faithful are accustomed to having clerics give the needed leadership. The laity are understandably hesitant to start their own elected councils, and the clergy get suspicious when they see the lay faithful move in that direction. We can also suspect some laypeople to be secretly happy and comfortable leaving the decisions and the responsibility to the clerics.

I cannot forget my discussion with a zealous Italian parish priest who was my friend. I asked him how his parish council functioned. (I did not even dare ask him if there was a laity council in his parish.) He replied in all seriousness and matter-of-factness: "Parish council? I am the parish council.

I love my people, and my people love me. I know what is good for them. I tell them what to do and they do it." I was convinced that he loved his people and that his people loved him. But his idea that there was no need for a parish council would have been right only if the parish had consisted solely of little children who had not reached adolescence, not in a parish with lay adults. And please note that this discussion was about a parish council, of which the parish priest would have been the chairman, and not yet about a laity council, where the chairman would be elected by the laity and the priest would be merely the chaplain!

The mistake that motivates these fears is equating "the Church" with the clergy and forgetting that the lay faithful comprise 99.9 percent of the Church. It is behaving as if the clerics had all the answers and had only to dispense them to the lay faithful. "Let the layman not imagine that his pastors are always such experts, that to every problem which arises, however complicated, they can readily give him a concrete solution, or even that such is their mission", declares the Second Vatican Council.[1] To continue to fear lay responsibility today is to ignore what the Council teaches us in *Lumen Gentium*, 31 to 37, which was earlier analyzed in this book. Not to appreciate the necessity of a specifically distinctive role for the laity is to promote a form of clericalism and to refuse to learn from history of the setback for the Church in some countries where clerical dominance in past ages has resulted in extreme reactions by some laypeople in our times.

[1] *Gaudium et Spes*, 43.

Seeing the lay apostolate
as power struggle

To stand for freedom, initiative and responsibility for the laity in the apostolate is not to promote a power struggle in the Church. To say that the laity should assume their own distinctive role is not to suggest that they should ignore the clergy or rival them or contend with them. It is simply to assert that the apostolate specific to the lay faithful is the Christianization of the temporal order as insiders, in the manner of leaven, salt or light. This is not the apostolate specific to the clergy.

A good and capable parish priest has nothing to fear from an active layperson who can deliver the goods in the secular area. They complement each other. They guarantee the presence and effectiveness of the Church in different arenas. If a cleric feels threatened by the competence of a layperson, we have to suspect that the cleric is somehow lacking in leadership, realism or humility, or in all three. And a layperson who regards the lay apostolate as a struggle to oust the clerics from positions of leadership has to be suspected of behaving like an adolescent. Growing young people tend to get unnecessarily argumentative toward their parents and want to challenge their authority, which they seem to regard as oppressive. They want to chart a new course for themselves, even if this means breaking a few customs along the way. And there are young people who seem to derive some pleasure from the embarrassment of their elders. Both clerics and laypeople need Christian maturity, good theology and acceptable spirituality based on the Gospel. The example set us by our Lord and Savior Jesus Christ is clear. When John and his brother James, with their mother lobbying for them, were striving to obtain the two top posts in the kingdom that Jesus was promising, Jesus called all his Apostles together and gave them a lesson on authority as service, not as domination: "You know that the rulers of the Gentiles lord it over them, and their great men exercise authority over them. It shall not be so among you; but whoever would be great among you must be your servant, and whoever would be first among you must be your slave; even as the Son of man came not to be served but to serve, and to give his life as a ransom for many" (Mt 20:25–28). In another context he taught them: "Whoever exalts himself will be humbled, and whoever humbles himself will be exalted" (Mt 23:12).

Incorrect ecclesiology

It follows that one reason for both hesitation and exaggeration regarding the need for responsibility and initiative in the lay apostolate is incorrect ecclesiology. It is important to see the Church as the communion of all the baptized in Jesus Christ. Baptism gives all the disciples of Christ a fundamental equality and a share in the general mission of the Church.

By the will of Christ, some men in the Church are ordained priests and bishops so that in the name of Christ, the Head of the Church, they may celebrate the sacred mysteries, preach the word of God and gather the people of God together. Therefore these clerics are called pastors. They are servants of all the baptized in the name of Christ. They do not lord it over the laity. They know that the laity are their brothers and sisters. With Saint Augustine they can say: "What I am for you terrifies me; what I am with you consoles me. For you I am a bishop; but with you I am a

Christian. The former is a title of duty; the latter, one of grace. The former is a danger; the latter, salvation."[2]

It is, therefore, a misunderstanding of the nature of the Church if some laypeople come together and say "We are Church" or call themselves the "Church from below". It is still a greater error if some laity go to the extreme of denying the necessity of priestly ordination and assert that laypeople can "preside" over the Eucharistic celebration when there is no priest around. It is wrong for the laity to imagine that they can set up and run parishes and preach. To say that some men have Holy Orders in the Church is not to assert that such men are necessarily holier before God, but only to say that, by the will of Christ, some men are ordained for the pastoral ministry to the whole body of believers. On the last day before God, we might be surprised to see who is holier than whom!

Both laypeople and clerics should therefore feel, think and speak of the Church as being all of us who are baptized in Christ. No layperson should treat Church matters as affairs of the clergy alone. That was how one layman behaved when the government was about to seize Church schools in my part of Nigeria. He came to me (I was the archbishop) and declared: "I hear that the government is going to take over your schools. This must not be allowed to happen. I have had my say. Now I am going away." I replied: "You are not going away. If the government is planning to seize *our* schools, Church schools, you are involved, because you are a member of the Church. So please sit down, and let us plan how to defend *our* schools."

---

[2] Saint Augustine, *Sermo* 340, 1: PL 38:1483; cf. also *Lumen Gentium*, 32.

Bishops are pastors;
laypeople are not pastors

Some clerics are afraid to promote greater responsibility for
the lay faithful in the apostolate because they think that such
a move tends to present laypeople as pastors. And there are
some lay faithful who appear to give some foundation for
such fears because they seem to see their organized associations as pressure groups within the Church. When such
laypeople hear that the laity are encouraged to study Holy
Scripture and theology, they secretly hope that there will
thus be a body of lay theologians who can urge the pope
and the bishops for a change in some elements of faith and
morals, such as the ordination of women, so-called birth
control and the possibility of a layperson "conducting" a
Eucharistic service in the absence of a priest. Such people
need good information on Church teaching regarding these
matters. And this teaching is rather clear.

Such moves and hopes would be a serious misunderstanding of the nature of the Church. Bishops and priests are ordained, and only they can validly consecrate bread and wine
into the Body and Blood of Christ and offer them to the
eternal Father. Only they can celebrate Mass. But all the baptized join and offer Christ to the Father by virtue of their
possession of the royal priesthood. They offer through and
with the ministerial or ordained priest.[3]

Bishops and priests are the pastors in the Church. This
is a question of sacramental designation through the Sacrament of Holy Orders. In the diocese, it is the bishop who
is the leader in the Church. In particular, he is the teacher
and pastor in questions of faith and morals. It is he who

[3] Cf. *Lumen Gentium*, 10.

authoritatively teaches the people what they are to believe
and what they are to do or not to do in order to attain salvation. In his main church, the bishop has his *cathedra*, the
seat symbolizing his teaching and pastoral ministry. And it
is he who is the liturgist, the leader of the diocese in the
public worship of the Church.

A lay theologian who explains the Catholic position on
some questions of faith and morals over the television is no
threat to the bishop and his priests. He is their brother and
"fellow worker for the kingdom of God" (cf. Col 4:11; Phil
2:25). But this is on condition that he remains faithful to orthodox Catholic teaching, of which the pope and the bishops
in communion with him are the authentic exponents, the
teaching authority in the Church, the Magisterium. That a
layperson knows and teaches theology is good and healthy
for Church and society. But that does not make the layperson a pastor.

The unity of the Church requires unity with the bishop
in doctrine and worship and unity of bishops with the pope.
It is damaged by the setting up of rival or parallel authorities. Unity of faith is not achieved by the use of pressure
groups or majority votes. When, however, a lay theologian
or canon law expert is well inserted into the faith and the
communion of charity which is the Church, then his witness in society is indeed precious for all.

Permanent urgency of
evangelizing the secular sphere

In spite of all the hesitations and possible risks, it remains
urgent for the lay faithful to be encouraged to evangelize
the secular sphere. It is a question of what is specific to the

lay apostolate. It is what the Second Vatican Council insists upon, especially in *Gaudium et Spes* (no. 43).

All this makes necessary, or at least very useful, the forming of laity councils that have the aim of promoting the apostolate of the laypeople in its many variations. It is such a council that can, for example, undertake action in the sociopolitical field when necessary. It can approach the political parties in a country or the government to urge the making of laws that respect God's plan, or the natural law, as the Catholic Church authoritatively interprets it. Suppose someone argues that the crucifix should be removed from the classroom or from the hospital ward or from the courtroom in a country that has been traditionally Catholic. Why can such a council not organize a demonstration in favor of retaining the crucifix? Why can it not conduct a campaign of protest letters to members of parliament to express the will of citizens who are Christians?

If anyone argues that laypeople cannot be expected to know the Catholic position on such matters, can one not answer that in this case the laity, and especially their leaders, should be better educated in their faith? Then they could foresee potential problems and take preemptive action or at least react adequately when necessary. If it is only the clergy who take the initiative in such matters, does this not indicate that some homework still needs to be done by the local Church? If the reason for hesitation is that the laity might thus set up a parallel church, then the reply is better formation and more careful organization as well as the selection of capable chaplains for the laity.

In all these and other reasons for hesitation in urging the laypeople to assume their own distinctive role, it has to be acknowledged that the risks are real and that therefore there are good grounds for hesitation. But the answer cannot be to abandon the whole attempt and to keep the lay apostolate as a mere participation in the apostolate of the clergy. What are needed are good theology, dynamic ecclesiology and the adequate formation of the lay faithful for their full participation in the general mission of the Church. These will be the concerns discussed in the rest of this book.

9

Complementary Roles in the Church

There are various roles and ministries in the Church. They are all necessary and complementary. If this is understood, it will be less difficult to understand and promote the specific apostolate that belongs to the lay faithful in the Church and in the world.

The Church is a communion

The Church, as has been mentioned above, is the communion of the baptized in Christ Jesus our Savior. It is he who makes the members of the Church brothers and sisters. He calls on all the baptized to be concerned and involved in the general mission of the Church, which is to spread the Good News of Jesus Christ: that all may know the one true God and Jesus Christ whom he has sent and that, believing in him and living the new life he merited for us, they may all at last attain salvation.

The Church is the new family of God, where the achievements of one member bring joy to all. The concern is not about status, not about who is greater than whom, but about whether Christ is known, loved and followed and whether the divine law is respected in the running of the earthly city.

"In the Church, there is diversity of service but unity of purpose."[1] All members of the Church do not have the

---

[1] *Apostolicam Actuositatem*, 2.

same type of role in the apostolate, but all apostolates are for the promotion of the one mission of the Church. *Lumen Gentium* is clear:

> By divine institution Holy Church is structured and governed with a wonderful diversity. "For just as in one body we have many members, yet all the members have not the same function, so we, the many, are one body in Christ, but severally members one of another" (Rom. 12:4–5). . . . If therefore everyone in the Church does not proceed by the same path, nevertheless all are called to sanctity and have received an equal privilege of faith through the justice of God (cf. 2 Pet. 1:1). And if by the will of Christ some are made teachers, dispensers of mysteries, and shepherds on behalf of others, yet all share a true equality with regard to the dignity and to the activity common to all the faithful for the building up of the Body of Christ.[2]

Diversity and complementarity in the Church need not threaten unity and harmony.

Bishops are teachers of the faith

Bishops are teachers of the faith. They guide the people in matters of faith and morals. They preach the Gospel to them without charge. Their immediate co-workers in this vital ministry are the priests. The lay faithful and the religious expect this service from their pastors and have the right to receive it.

"Bishops, to whom is assigned the task of ruling the Church of God", says the Second Vatican Council, "should, together with their priests, so preach the message of Christ that all the earthly activities of the faithful will be bathed

[2] *Lumen Gentium*, 32.

in the light of the gospel. All pastors should remember too that by their daily conduct and concern they are revealing the face of the Church to the world."[3]

Through his teaching office, and also through the liturgy and general pastoral approach, the bishop in the diocese helps and animates the various vocations in the Church to carry out with joy and efficiency their own share in the mission of the Church. He, moreover, promotes harmony and love between them. Priests live and work as the immediate co-workers of the bishop. Religious make their own contribution by living with authenticity and credibility their life of manifesting the power of God's grace in the following of Christ according to the three evangelical counsels of chastity, poverty and obedience. And the lay faithful do their part by bringing the spirit of the Gospel into the various sectors of secular life.

"The laity have the right, as do all Christians", says the Second Vatican Council, "to receive in abundance from their sacred pastors the spiritual goods of the Church, especially the assistance of the Word of God and the sacraments."[4] If this happens, and if the laity respond with competence and perseverance, there is hope that the Gospel will be more and more active in animating society. And the Church will thus be rendering more credible witness to Christ. Pope Benedict XVI said to the members of the International Pontifical Theological Commission on December 2, 2011: "The social commitment of the Church is not just something human, nor is it reduced to a social theory. The transformation of society brought about by Christians over centuries is in answer to the coming of the Son of God into the world: the

---

[3] *Gaudium et Spes*, 43.
[4] *Lumen Gentium*, 37.

splendor of such Truth and Love illumines every culture and society."[5]

Diocesan programs should not rule out initiative

Every diocese has the right, and even the duty, to have its program, its policy, its way of coordinating the different apostolates. The temptation to rigidity should be resisted. The diocesan program should not be so tightly structured that little or no room is left for the surprises of the Holy Spirit. The Spirit breathes where he wills. He can give his charisms to unlikely people and at times when the diocesan officials are not expecting it. Diocesan directors of the various offices should not look askance at new apostolic proposals just because these were not initiated by them. Jealousy and envy are always possible temptations. The Gospel of Mark supplies us with a fascinating example and shows how Jesus handled it: "John said to him, 'Teacher, we saw a man casting out demons in your name, and we forbade him, because he was not following us.' But Jesus said, 'Do not forbid him; for no one who does a mighty work in my name will be able soon after to speak evil of me. For he that is not against us is for us'" (Mk 9:38–40).

Diocesan officials should also avoid putting the bishop at the center, as if he were to occupy the place of Christ. Temptations to flattery, sycophancy and personality cult from both clergy and religious or also the laity are always possible. The bishop should do all in his power to discourage such a waste of apostolic energy.

Clerics should by the study of good theology and eccle-

---

[5] Papal address in *L'Osservatore Romano*, weekly English ed. December 21, 2011, p. 15.

siology appreciate the place of the laity and the importance of the lay apostolate, which is not based on the scarcity of priests or because many priests are overworked. The apostolate of the lay faithful belongs to true ecclesiology, to the essence of what the Church is and should be doing. It will always be needed, even when and where priestly vocations are abundant. The lay faithful are not simply for emergency use by clerics.

Set up diocesan pastoral study, formation and retreat centers

A diocese reaps great dividends if it has a center where groups, big and small, can come for pastoral reflection, theological updating, formation for various apostolates, and spiritual retreats. Such a center needs a director who is a credit to the Church, who is hopefully an experienced pastor or good theologian, who is a capable organizer, and who has a sharp eye for spotting the most talented experts or witnesses to invite to meet a group. People who are controversial figures, who are incurable protesters in the Church or who think of setting up their own parallel magisterium alongside that of the pope and the bishops are not good prospects for such a vital assignment. Major seminaries and Catholic universities will often be able to offer personnel who can animate encounters in such centers.

The Fathers of the Second Vatican Council speak of the importance of "unremitting study" so that "dialogue with the world and with people of all shades of opinion"[6] can be established. A pastoral center can be a forum for this, on condition that it is directed by a person who loves the Church and who is well informed.

[6] *Gaudium et Spes*, 43.

Pope Benedict XVI encouraged the setting up of a center to promote the lay apostolate: "Laypeople have an important role to play in the Church and in society. To enable them properly to take up this role, it is fitting that centers of biblical, spiritual, liturgical and pastoral formation be organized in the dioceses."[7]

A diocesan pastoral center can also help the bishop and his assistants, including the lay faithful, to assess what is positive and negative in the various areas of Church life and to seek remedies for any defects. "It does not escape the Church how great a distance lies between the message she offers and the human failings of those to whom the gospel is entrusted."[8]

Set up laity councils

No one person, no matter how wise, can do the work of the apostolate alone in matters that concern many people. Experience has proved that concerted action in councils or similar arrangements is useful, even necessary. The Second Vatican Council advises that councils be set up to answer local needs in various areas: "In dioceses, as far as possible, there should be councils which assist the apostolic work of the Church either in the field of making the gospel known and men holy, or in the charitable, social or other spheres. To this end, clergy and religious should appropriately cooperate with the laity."[9]

Situations vary much around the world, and no one way of responding to these situations should be imposed everywhere indiscriminately. Experience in some places has

[7] *Africae Munus*, 128.

[8] *Gaudium et Spes*, 43.

[9] *Apostolicam Actuositatem*, 26.

shown that parish councils can coordinate the entire mission of the Church in the parish, under the direction of the parish priest. And there can be a corresponding diocesan council over which the bishop presides. Such councils are concerned with evangelization in its full extent: the ministry of priests, sacramental administration, catechesis, *missio ad gentes*, new evangelization or re-evangelization, the religious life in all its forms, and the lay apostolate in its fullness.

To coordinate the lay apostolate and encourage it in many forms, experience has also shown that it can be helpful to set up specifically lay apostolate councils. Such councils promote harmony between the lay associations and groups, encourage initiative among them, spearhead action on the social, cultural and political levels by the laity, and assure unity with the clergy and the religious and obedience to the bishop. Such councils can be on the parish, diocesan, regional or national level. At the national level, the reference relationship is with the Catholic bishops' conference.

Membership in such councils is for the laity only and is generally by election. In the diocese, the bishop approves the constitution or statutes. At the national level, this falls to the bishops' conference. It is beneficial for the bishop to promote a good deal of dialogue, discussion and consultation before the statutes are finalized. And a limited term of office is desirable for each officeholder, so that no one remains in the same position endlessly, without an honorable method of introducing a change of personnel. Occasional change is healthy, because it helps to avoid attachment, personality cult and stagnation, and it promotes the formation of more and more people in leadership. The bishop may also find it wise to approve the constitution initially for a trial period of a few years, so that there will be a smooth way to learn from experience and make amendments.

Some projects or initiatives affect the whole Church in a diocese or even a country and demand careful and discreet discussion with the bishop or the bishops' conference before they are undertaken. This can apply to matters relating to socio-political action by the laity. Moreover, care should be taken to distinguish between initiatives that laypeople take on their individual responsibility and action that they undertake in the name of the Church.

The role of the priest chaplain to a lay apostolate council has great importance and will be discussed shortly.

Set up associations for Catholic professional groups

Catholic professionals such as doctors, lawyers, teachers, business people, politicians and journalists are all called upon, as is every baptized person, to witness to Christ, not only in their private lives but also in their various professions. It can be a great help to the individual professional if a lay apostolate association for his profession exists. In such an association, the teaching of the Church on matters focusing on the profession in question can be examined in depth, studied, reflected upon, and prayed over. Challenges that a Catholic of that profession meets in actual work situations can be examined.

It has therefore been found useful to have a Catholic medical association, a Catholic teachers' association, a Catholic legal practitioners' association, and so on. It is not the aim to make these associations into trade unions. No. They are purely Catholic associations to favor the apostolate according to the Gospel and to help the Catholic professional practice his faith in his profession. When such an association is set up for Catholics in politics or government, it must be made clear that the aim is not to support one political party or another or one particular government, but simply to help Catholics live the faith in the political arena.

Associations of this type may find that it is helpful occasionally to invite well-prepared theologians, pastors or other experts to share with them a detailed study on a theme that touches their profession in particular. A lecture can be followed by questions and answers and can awaken the desire to promote further study. If there is no suitable library that the professionals can consult, at least there can be contact with the diocesan bookshop to procure the desirable Catholic books. To be especially recommended to Catholic professionals are the Bible, the *Catechism of the Catholic Church* and the *Compendium of the Social Doctrine of the Church.*

These Catholic professional associations can help new members of their profession by allowing them to benefit from the experience of their elder colleagues in living their faith in their profession. The members will also be of particular help to parish and diocesan pastoral councils. They are generally respected people in society who have to their credit many years of devoted service and social credibility as good citizens.

Catholic professional association members can also ask themselves what they can do for the wider society. Among the possibilities are newspaper articles, television programs in which matters of the moment are discussed, professional help to the poor who cannot generally pay for such services and proposals to political parties and governments.

A Catholic professional association should request the bishop to assign it a learned man of God as chaplain.[10]

---

[10] Cf. *Africae Munus*, 138.

The role of a lay apostolate chaplain

A lay apostolate council or association is an important group in the Church. Its action affects many people. It is important that its officers and members be well equipped with the best of doctrine that the Church can offer. They should also be sustained by the spiritual nourishment that the sacraments give.

These and other reasons have traditionally convinced bishops to appoint chaplains to lay apostolate organizations. It is best if such chaplains are priests who are well versed in sacred theology and who have personal pastoral experience. It is clear that they should not be problem priests or those who tend to be obsessive about some particular issue. They should faithfully transmit the teaching of the Catholic Church, introduce the lay faithful to Church documents such as those named above and celebrate the sacraments for them.

The chaplain is not the leader of the lay apostolate council. He is its link with the bishop to guarantee ecclesial communion. But he should allow the laypeople to elect their leaders, and he should willingly work with them. Obviously, it is for him to advise them about and sometimes teach them Church doctrine. In matters that are not doctrinal but rather prudential, and in questions regarding choices in the secular sphere, he should leave them the freedom to function on their own. Where it is necessary to get directives from the bishop because of pastoral or other implications, he should know how to proceed with the needed prudence and respect for all sides.

The Fathers of the Second Vatican Council showed great interest in the role of these chaplains and went into considerable detail:

Particular attention must be paid to the selection of priests who are capable of promoting particular forms of the apostolate of the laity and are properly trained. By virtue of the mission they receive from the hierarchy, those who are engaged in this ministry represent the hierarchy by their pastoral activity. Always adhering faithfully to the spirit and teaching of the Church, they should promote proper relations between laity and hierarchy. They should devote themselves to nourishing the spiritual life and an apostolic mentality in the Catholic societies entrusted to them; they should contribute their wise counsel to the apostolic activity of these associations and promote their undertakings. Through continuous dialogue with the laity, these priests should carefully search for the forms which make apostolic activity more fruitful. They should promote the spirit of unity within the association as well as between it and others.[11]

The importance of the role of the university Catholic chaplain needs to be stressed. Blessed John Paul II, in his Apostolic Constitution *Ex Corde Ecclesiae*, on Catholic universities, says how important it is that "Catholic members of this community will be offered opportunities to assimilate Catholic teaching and practice into their lives and will be encouraged to participate in the celebration of the sacraments, especially the Eucharist as the most perfect act of community worship."[12] It is the university chaplain who should give leadership in this. He will need the collaboration perhaps of other priests and religious and certainly of the laypersons, especially the academic staff.[13]

From the above considerations, it is clear that the promotion of the apostolate of the laity demands the cooperation of all

[11] *Apostolicam Actuositatem*, 25.

[12] *Ex Corde Ecclesiae*, 39.

[13] Cf. ibid., art 6, §2.

in the Church: the bishops, the priests, the religious and, of course, the laypeople themselves, especially their leaders. The unity and diversity for which the Church is known show that the different roles are complementary. What is required of each member of the Church is fidelity to that person's role.

Theology on the Laity and Lay Spirituality

The reflections made so far contain elements relating to a theology on the laity and to lay spirituality. But now it seems proper to focus directly on these two related themes. They are indispensable supports for an authentic lay apostolate.

Some indications of the need to spell out this theology

From time to time one meets clerics, religious or laypeople who show signs of being unclear about the theology on the laity in the Church. But good theology is important for an authentic apostolate. The more clearly it is understood who the layperson is, the easier it will be to understand what engagement in the mission of the Church is to be expected from that person.

There are some people in the Church who, without expressly saying so, look on the lay apostolate as an extension of the clerical apostolate or as a mandate given to the laity by the Church, and they understand the Church to be the bishops and the priests.

There are some laypeople who think that by involvement in the mission of the Church they are merely helping their parish priest or bishop. They think that if, as laypeople, they are married in Church, come to Sunday Mass and pay their Church dues, they are already doing much as good Christians and should be recognized as such by the clergy. Implicitly, they identify the Church with the clergy and regard the laypeople as the flock to be cared for by the Church, to be blessed and to be congratulated and recognized when they help in some Church work. They speak of the clergy as "they" and of the laity as "us".

The fact that medical doctors and legal experts often use the term "laymen" to refer to people not in their profession reinforces this popular belief that in the Church "laypeople" are the clients of the clerics who are regarded as the real insiders, as the Church. There is also a popular saying that there are three traditional professions: medicine, law and the Church. And by Church is meant clerics!

These are some of the reasons that make it imperative to have greater clarity about the theological meaning of the layperson in the Church.

Life in Christ

By faith and Baptism we are incorporated into Christ and the Church. "Through Baptism we are freed from sin and reborn as sons of God; we become members of Christ, are incorporated into the Church and made sharers in her mission."[1] "Baptism not only purifies from all sins, but also makes the neophyte 'a new creature,' an adopted son of God, who has become a 'partaker of the divine nature,' member

---

[1] *Catechism of the Catholic Church*, 2nd ed. (Libreria Editrice Vaticana and United States Catholic Conference, 1997) (hereafter CCC), 1213.

of Christ and co-heir with him, and a temple of the Holy Spirit."[2]

To become a member of the Church is to become "one in Christ" (Gal 3:28) with other baptized people. The Church is communion with Christ and with his members, the baptized. "I am the vine, you are the branches. He who abides in me, and I in him, he it is that bears much fruit, for apart from me you can do nothing" (Jn 15:5). "The communion of Christians with Jesus has the communion of God as Trinity, namely, the unity of the Son to the Father in the gift of the Holy Spirit, as its model and source, and is itself the means to achieve this communion", says Blessed John Paul II.[3] Saint Cyprian therefore writes that the Church shines forth as "a people made one with the unity of the Father, Son and Holy Spirit".[4]

The Holy Spirit gives the Church "a unity of fellowship and service", says the Second Vatican Council. "He furnishes and directs her with various gifts, both hierarchical and charismatic, and adorns her with the fruits of his grace."[5]

By the will of Christ, some men are made pastors in the Church. These are the bishops and the priests who are ordained to serve the rest in the name of Christ. All in the Church, both pastors and the lay faithful, and also the religious, "share a true equality with regard to the dignity and to the activity common to all the faithful for the building up of the Body of Christ".[6]

The lay apostolate, like all apostolates in the Church, is

---

[2] CCC 1265.

[3] *Christifideles Laici*, 18.

[4] Saint Cyprian, *De orat. Dom.* 23: PL 4:553.

[5] *Lumen Gentium*, 4.

[6] Ibid., 32.

carried out in the consciousness that the whole Church is a communion. As Blessed John Paul II puts it: "Precisely because it derives *from* Church *communion*, the sharing of the lay faithful in the threefold mission of Christ requires that it be lived and realized *in communion* and *for the increase of communion itself.*"[7] In the life of union with Christ, prayer has a very important place. The layperson will do well to pay great attention to liturgical prayer and also to personal prayer. Saint Thérèse of Lisieux testifies: "For me, prayer is a surge of the heart; it is a simple look turned toward heaven; it is a cry of gratitude and of love, in the midst of both trial and joy."[8]

The lay faithful in the Church

The lay faithful are those Christians who by Baptism are incorporated into Christ and the Church and who are sent to give witness to Christ in the secular sphere. This secular character is specific to the laity because it designates who they are in Christ. It therefore spells out what their apostolate should be.

The laity are called to penetrate and perfect the temporal sphere of things through the spirit of the Gospel.[9] They "exercise [their] apostolate in the world as a kind of leaven".[10] This right and duty are derived from Baptism, which unites them with Christ. They are strengthened by the Holy Spirit at Confirmation and nourished by the Holy Eucharist. If

---

[7] *Christifideles Laici*, 14; italics in the original.

[8] Thérèse of Lisieux, *Manuscrits autobiographiques*, C 25r. in Oeuvres completes (Paris: Cerf and Desclée de Brouwer, 1992), p. 268.

[9] Cf. *Apostolicam Actuositatem*, 2.

[10] Ibid.

they are married, they receive further graces characteristic of the Sacrament of Matrimony. They are consecrated into a royal priesthood and a holy people (cf. 1 Pet 2:4–10), so that they may offer spiritual sacrifices through everything they do and witness to Christ in the midst of the world. They thus carry out their apostolate through faith, hope and charity.[11]

Most adult lay faithful are married. The family is of central importance in their lives as followers of Christ. The Second Vatican Council calls the family "the domestic Church".[12] It is in it and through it that the spouses grow as persons and as Christians. They become parents and are the first preachers of the faith to their children. It is the family that helps the members, parents and children, to grow in communion, in mutual forgiveness and in openness to other families and people in need, to learn to be good citizens and to contribute as members of the Church. The importance of the family in living one's faith in Christ and witnessing to him should never be underestimated.

Universal call to holiness

Inaugurating the Kingdom of God, Jesus in the Sermon on the Mount invites all his followers to perfection: "You, therefore, must be perfect, as your heavenly Father is perfect" (Mt 5:48).

The Second Vatican Council is not ambiguous: "All the faithful of Christ of whatever rank or status are called to the fullness of the Christian life and to the perfection of charity. By this holiness a more human way of life is promoted

---

[11] Ibid., 3.
[12] *Lumen Gentium*, 11; cf. *Apostolicam Actuositatem*, 11.

even in this earthly society."[13] In paragraph 41 of this same Dogmatic Constitution, the Council spells out how this life of holiness or perfection is lived by each Christian according to the person's state of life or vocation: bishops, priests, other ministers, married couples, laborers and consecrated religious. It concludes: "All of Christ's faithful, therefore, whatever be the conditions, duties and circumstances of their lives, will grow in holiness day by day through these very situations, if they accept all of them with faith from the hand of their heavenly Father, and if they cooperate with the divine will by showing every man through their earthly activities the love with which God has loved the world."

For the lay faithful, not only should family concerns and other secular affairs not be excluded from their life of holiness, but these are the precise areas where they are called to perfection and holiness. It is from a holy life that we can talk of a fruitful apostolate in any state of life. "Holiness, then, must be called a fundamental presupposition and an irreplaceable condition for everyone in fulfilling the mission of salvation within the Church."[14]

Growing signs of a quest for deeper lay spirituality

There are encouraging signs of a quest for greater depth in lay spirituality in our times. More and more laypeople are gathering to participate in activities that will help them discover, explore, and enrich that spirituality. Members of lay movements and associations meet for days of Scripture study, prayer and reflection on Church documents in or-

---

[13] *Lumen Gentium*, 40.
[14] *Christifideles Laici*, 17.

der to understand better and live that spirituality specific to the lay faithful. Pastoral, retreat and conference centers have served the Church well by providing favorable climates for this reflection.

The Congregation for the Causes of Saints in the Vatican is also to be congratulated for the greater attention it gives to the promotion of the causes of the lay faithful. Dioceses and lay associations that originate these causes need to be encouraged. Seeing that the majority of canonized saints are religious or clerics, the beatification or canonization of laypeople is a way for the Church to declare, without words, that the call to holiness is universal and is for all states of life in the Church. We thank God that we have had the canonization of Saint Maria Goretti, eleven-year-old martyr to chastity (Italy), Saint Thomas More, public official, martyr (England), the twenty-two Martyrs of Uganda, martyrs to chastity, and Saint Kateri Tekakwitha, laywoman (Canada and the United States), and the beatification of Victoria Rasoamanarivo, wife, widow and devoted Church worker (Madagascar), Luigi and Maria Beltrame-Quattrocchi, model spouses (Italy), Louis and Zélie-Marie Martin, parents of Saint Thérèse of Lisieux, model spouses (France), Pier Giorgio Frassati, young medical doctor (Italy), Isidore Bakanja, twenty-four-year-old houseboy and voluntary catechist, martyr (Democratic Republic of the Congo), David Okelo and Gildo Irwa, young martyrs (Uganda), Chiara Luce Badano, eighteen-year-old Focolare member (Italy), Hildegard Burjan, wife, widow and foundress of a congregation of women religious (Austria) and others. All these are lay faithful who lived in perfection and holiness in their respective areas of life.

Saint Francis de Sales on the
spirituality suitable for laypeople

In his classical work, *The Introduction to the Devout Life*, written almost four hundred years ago, Saint Francis de Sales outlines beautifully the spirituality or way of holiness suitable to the laity. What he calls devotion we might call holiness or spirituality. The heart of his teaching is that spirituality has to be lived in different ways according to a person's vocation and mission. We quote him at length.

> When God the Creator made all things, he commanded the plants to bring forth fruit each according to its own kind; he has likewise commanded Christians, who are the living plants of his Church, to bring forth the fruits of devotion, each one in accord with his character, his station and his calling.
>
> I say that devotion must be practiced in different ways by the nobleman and by the working man, by the servant and by the prince, by the widow, by the unmarried girl and by the married woman. But even this distinction is not sufficient; for the practice of devotion must be adapted to the strength, to the occupation and to the duties of each one in particular.
>
> Tell me, please, my Philothea, whether it is proper for a bishop to want to lead a solitary life like a Carthusian, or for married people to be no more concerned than a Capuchin about increasing their income; or for a working man to spend his whole day in church like a religious; or on the other hand for a religious to be constantly exposed like a bishop to all the events and circumstances that bear on the needs of our neighbor. Is not this sort of devotion ridiculous, unorganized and intolerable? Yet this absurd error oc-

curs very frequently, but in no way does true devotion, my Philothea, destroy anything at all. On the contrary, it perfects and fulfills all things. In fact if it ever works against, or is inimical to, anyone's legitimate station and calling, then it is very definitely false devotion. . . .

Moreover, just as every sort of gem, cast in honey, becomes brighter and more sparkling, each according to its color, so each person becomes more acceptable and fitting in his own vocation when he sets his vocation in the context of devotion. Through devotion your family cares become more peaceful, mutual love between husband and wife becomes more sincere, the service we owe to the prince becomes more faithful, and our work, no matter what it is, becomes more pleasant and agreeable.

It is therefore an error and even a heresy to wish to exclude the exercise of devotion from military divisions, from the artisans' shops, from the courts of princes, from family households. I acknowledge, my dear Philothea, that the type of devotion which is purely contemplative, monastic and religious can certainly not be exercised in these sorts of stations and occupations, but besides this threefold type of devotion, there are many others fit for perfecting those who live in a secular state.

Therefore, in whatever situation we happen to be, we can and we must aspire to the life of perfection.[15]

Saint Francis de Sales has said it all: Let the laypeople take on their own distinctive spirituality in order to live authentic lives as Christians and witness to Christ in the secular world.

---

[15] *The Introduction to the Devout Life*, part 1, chapter 3, as quoted in the Liturgy of the Hours, Office of Readings for January 24.

Living a lay spirituality

Consequent on what has so far been discussed, the layperson should strive to live a healthy and robust lay spirituality.

Jesus Christ, our Savior, sent by his eternal Father, is the fountain and source of the whole apostolate of the Church. Therefore, the success of a layperson in the apostolate depends on that person's living union with Christ. Jesus has told us to abide in him so that we can bear fruit (cf. Jn 15:5). This life of intimate union with Christ in the Church is nourished by spiritual aids that are common to all the baptized, especially attentive and prayerful reading of the Bible and participation in the sacred liturgy.

The laity are to make a vital synthesis between these spiritual aids and the fulfillment of their secular duties in the family, place of work and in society as a whole. They make progress in holiness through these secular duties, not in spite of them. Saint Paul tells the Colossians: "Whatever you do, in word or deed, do everything in the name of the Lord Jesus, giving thanks to God the Father through him" (Col 3:17).

Laypeople are to strive to make correct judgments about the true meaning and value of things of this world, both in themselves and in their relation to a person's final end. Laypeople are to go through life as a pilgrimage. They are to aspire to the riches that last forever and generously dedicate their entire lives to spreading God's Kingdom and perfecting the sphere of earthly things, according to the spirit of Christ. They are to strive to do good to everyone, especially to those of the household of the faith (cf. Gal 6:10), put aside all malice and thus draw people to Christ and his Gospel.

They are to follow Jesus, who was humble and poor, and they are to be ready to suffer persecution for his sake.

Laypeople who live like that are giving witness to Christ, each according to his status in life as single, married or widowed. Competence in one's profession is also part of this life of service and witness. Attention to the social virtues that distinguish a good citizen: honesty, justice, sincerity, kindness and courage, are not to be forgotten.

The above are some of the elements of sound lay spirituality listed by the Second Vatican Council, which puts before the laity the example set by the Blessed Virgin Mary. She led a life in situations similar to what many people at that time faced; she had family concerns and labors and was always intimately united with her Son. Thus she cooperated in the work of the Savior in a manner that was altogether unique. Laypeople should devoutly venerate her and commend their life and apostolate to her motherly concern.[16]

Witness value of the life of a convinced lay apostle

The witness value of the life of a layperson who lives the authentic lay spirituality in the apostolate is very great. As Pope Paul VI observes: "Modern man listens more willingly to witnesses than to teachers, and if he does listen to teachers, it is because they are witnesses."[17] Example convinces more than words. It is primarily by conduct and life, rather than by words, that the layperson will bring the spirit of Christ to the secular order. His life of holiness, of fidelity

[16] Cf. *Apostolicam Actuositatem*, 4.

[17] Address to the members of the *Consilium de Laicis* on October 2, 1974; also quoted in *Evangelii Nuntiandi*, 41.

to the Gospel and of witness to Christ cannot go without effect.

"Being a Christian is not the result of an ethical choice or a lofty idea, but the encounter with an event, a person, which gives life a new horizon and a decisive direction."[18] "The real novelty of the New Testament lies not so much in new ideas as in the figure of Christ himself, who gives flesh and blood to those concepts."[19]

A layperson who has encountered Jesus Christ in this living way and who lives this event wholeheartedly, is bound to make a lasting impact in the spheres of the secular order in which he is engaged. And sometimes the witness of such a layperson can have a greater effect on people in the world than can a similar witness from a cleric or a religious, because laypeople identify more easily with laypeople who share with them similar circumstances of life in the secular world. This makes it all the more important for laypersons, living the richness of their theological and ecclesiological heritage, to assume their own distinctive role.

---

[18] *Deus Caritas Est*, 1.
[19] Ibid., 12.

11

Ecclesial Movements and
New Communities

Ecclesial movements and new communities are important realities in the Church of our times. They deserve more focused reflection. They are fresh and emergent ways in which many laypeople are doing their best to live an authentic theology of the laity as enunciated by the Second Vatican Council. They generally have robust spiritualities. Our reflections cannot be complete without striving to listen to what the Holy Spirit may be telling us through them.

The nature of the ecclesial movements
and new communities

The ecclesial movements and new communities are of many types and colors. They are generally comprised of the lay faithful, although some of them make room for priests and religious who share the same general spirit. Here we are examining them as concrete efforts of the laity to live the dynamic theology of the Second Vatican Council on the Church and, more particularly, on the place and apostolate of laypeople in the Church and in the world. Although, therefore, in the strict sense, one could speak of the Franciscans in the thirteenth century or of the Mendicant Orders in general as new ecclesial movements or new communities, here we are focusing on those realities which have arisen in the Church largely in the last half century.

The climate in which these movements and communities arose is that largely influenced by the Second Vatican Council along with some of its dynamic concepts, such as Church as family of God, as communion expressed in mission and as a kind of sacrament of intimate union with God and of the unity of mankind. The Council also spoke of the Holy Spirit giving his charisms as he wishes, of the duty of pastors not indeed to quench the Spirit, but to discern the spirits and to hold onto what is good. The Council, therefore, underlined the place of diversity and complementarity in the Church, which need not threaten unity, and of the need for participation and co-responsibility in the apostolate to which everyone in the Church is called. The laypeople are in particular called to evangelize the secular sphere so that the Church can be sufficiently present in those areas.

Reflecting on these and similar teachings of the Second Vatican Council, several associations, movements or communities of laypeople have been asking themselves how they can better witness to Christ in the world of today. They are also concerned that the so-called "postmodern" world is tending more and more to exclude God from life. They are aware that without God there is no hope for mankind.[1] They know that "without the Creator the creature would disappear."[2] The ecclesial movements and new communities therefore strive to offer their members a dynamic experience of a personal encounter with Christ, the Lord and Master. They are aware that he said to his first disciples:

---

[1] Cf. Benedict XVI, Encyclical Letter *Spe Salvi*, 3.
[2] *Gaudium et Spes*, 36.

"Come and see" (Jn 1:39). They seek to propose an encounter that changes a person's life. They provide an initiation to personal prayer. They propose a concrete apostolate. They have good approaches to the family and the education of young people. They want to live the Church as communion and to harmonize their work with the other realities in the Church. For several reasons, I refrain from giving a list of them or of proposing some as models. As was mentioned earlier in this book, in 2006 the Pontifical Council for the Laity published a *Directory of International Associations of the Faithful* approved by it on the universal Church level. Some of them, but not all, could be regarded as ecclesial movements or new communities. But we do not exclude from these reflections those that function only in one diocese or nation.

Charismatic renewal movements

Charismatic movements show special attention to the gifts or charisms of the Holy Spirit and stress "Baptism in the Spirit", prayer in the Spirit, healing and speaking in tongues. The charismatic movement began among Protestants. Catholics came to be involved in it only about fifty years ago. The movement takes many forms. Within the Catholic Church, it is now found in forms that raise no problems and are accepted and recommended. Many regard it as an opportunity for the Church. In Italy there is an association, Renewal in the Holy Spirit, at both the diocesan and national levels that has received due ecclesiastical approval.

Pastors of the Church should realize that, if well conducted, Catholic charismatic renewal movements are not part of the problem of the exodus of Catholics from the Church but rather part of the solution. Many members of these movements remain faithful to the Church because of the movements, because they find in the Church what others were looking for outside of the Church. What is very important is that they teach people to read the Bible, to meditate on it and to pray with it. The various communities that have sprung up from within the charismatic movement in the last fifty years are at the front line of service to the Church and to the spread of the Gospel, even though we have to admit that some people drift away in any case.

What the charismatic renewal groups need is good leadership, suitable translations of the Bible approved by the bishops' conference, guidance in Bible reading and initiation into personal and (non-liturgical) group prayer. Supplied with these, they can concentrate on learning from Scripture readings how to bear suffering, setbacks and sickness and how to look on the acquisition of earthly goods: in short, how to follow Christ in the world of today. And they need to be motivated to evangelize others, to share the Good News of salvation in Jesus Christ.

Papal encouragement

The popes of our time have encouraged ecclesial movements and new communities and given directives as to how they can best be cared for in order to produce the most desirable results. Let us quote Blessed John Paul II and Pope Benedict XVI.

In his homily on the vigil of Pentecost, May 25, 1996, Blessed John Paul II saw the movements as "one of the gifts of the Spirit for our times and a reason for hope for the Church and for mankind".

In his message to the participants at the World Congress of Ecclesial Movements, May 27–29, 1998, the same Holy Father wrote: "There is no conflict or opposition in the

Church between the *institutional dimension* and the *charismatic dimension*, of which movements are a significant expression. Both are co-essential to the divine constitution of the Church founded by Jesus, because they both help to make the mystery of Christ and his saving work present in the world."[3]

Even before he became pope, Cardinal Joseph Ratzinger, as Prefect of the Congregation for the Doctrine of the Faith, presented a rich theological analysis of these movements and communities at the meeting of Blessed John Paul II with them on May 30, 1998. As Pope Benedict XVI, he met a large group of the faithful representing more than one hundred new lay associations on June 3, 2006, and said that the ecclesial movements and the new communities and their experience are a "luminous sign of the beauty of Christ and of the Church, his Bride".

His positive assessment and encouragement of these realities continued in his address to the participants at the seminar for bishops organized by the Pontifical Council for the Laity, on May 17, 2008. He said that

> The Ecclesial Movements and New Communities are one of the most important innovations inspired by the Holy Spirit in the Church for the implementation of the Second Vatican Council. . . . Paul VI and John Paul II were able to welcome and discern, to encourage and promote the unexpected explosion of the new lay realities which in various and surprising forms have restored vitality, faith and hope to the whole Church. Indeed, even then they were already bearing witness to the joy, reasonableness and beauty of being Christian, showing that they were grateful for belonging to the mystery of communion which is the Church.[4]

[3] Quoted in Pontifical Council for the Laity, *Pastors and the Ecclesial Movements*, 2009, p. 26.

[4] In ibid., p. 16.

Ecclesial movements and new communities and the local Church

The relationship between the bishops and the ecclesial movements and new communities in their dioceses is important for the life of the Church. Pope Benedict XVI summarized the desirable attitude on the part of bishops in what he said to a group of German bishops in an *ad limina* visit: "I . . . ask you to approach movements very lovingly" (November 18, 2006). Bishops are expected to study the statutes of these movements. The bishops, the pope says, will "understand that the Ecclesial Movements and New Communities are not an additional problem or risk that comes to top our already difficult task. No! They are a gift of the Lord, a valuable resource for enriching the entire Christian Community with their charisms." Pope Benedict lists "the many gifts they bear, which we have learned to recognize and appreciate: missionary enthusiasm, effective courses of Christian formation, a witness of faithfulness and obedience to the Church, sensitivity to the needs of the poor and a wealth of vocations."[5]

Bishops and their diocesan officials, by patient and loving dialogue, will find out ways to insert these movements and communities better into the diocesan family and to promote harmony between them and the clergy, religious and other lay apostolate groups. And when correction becomes necessary, it is not impossible to make it in a way that it is likely to be accepted. Pope Benedict XVI said to the Roman Clergy on February 22, 2007: "If the Lord gives us new gifts we must be grateful, even if at times they may be inconvenient. And it is beautiful that without an initiative of the hierarchy

[5] Address of May 17, 2008, in ibid., p. 17.

but with an initiative from below, as people say, but which also truly comes from on High, that is, as a gift of the Holy Spirit, new forms of life are being born in the Church just as, moreover they were born down the ages."[6]

The ecclesial movements and new communities also have duties to the local Church that must be fulfilled if the best results are to be achieved. The leaders of these movements have a key role in accomplishing this. They should regard themselves as children of the Church. They should resist temptations to exclusivism and a tendency to absolutize their own experiences and to try unwittingly to set up a church parallel to the parish or the diocese. Pope Benedict XVI touched on this point when he was addressing the people of Rome Diocese during their Ecclesial Convention on May 26, 2009: "I would like to ask the movements and communities that came into being after the Second Vatican Council and that in our Diocese too are a precious gift for which we must always thank the Lord . . . always to ensure that their formation processes lead their members to develop a true sense of belonging to the parish community."[7]

Pride and an attitude of being superior to others and the presumption that one's movement is the best and the only valid answer to the needs of the Church are also possible temptations for the movements and new communities. Moreover, it is for the leader or founder of a movement to discourage totally any personality cult detected among the members. Blessed John Paul II lists criteria for the discernment of the ecclesial nature of lay groups in general. It would be useful for leaders of ecclesial movements and new communities to bear these in mind and to see how they apply

[6] Quoted in ibid., p. 32.
[7] Address in *L'Osservatore Romano*, weekly English ed. June 3, 2009, p. 4.

to their own groups. Here are the five criteria that the pope mentions: the primacy given to the call of every Christian to holiness, the responsibility of professing the Catholic faith, the witness to a strong and authentic communion, conformity to and participation in the Church's apostolic goals, and a commitment to a presence in human society. With such fundamental criteria, good fruits can be hoped for.[8]

Fruits to be hoped for from the ecclesial movements and new communities

Where the ecclesial movements and new communities function well, there are good fruits that one can hope to reap. These movements and communities can help the local Church avoid the mentality of being a "maintenance Church" by bringing with them the freshness of missionary enthusiasm rather than an attitude of "business as usual". Within the same diocese, even in a country of long-standing evangelization, there are always people who have not been reached with the Good News of salvation in Jesus Christ. And in the world of today, with the widespread facility for quick travel and instant communication, even believers in other religions and nonbelievers can be found in the same area.

Pope Benedict XVI often stressed the importance of new evangelization. Many areas that have been traditionally Christian now have many people who in practice are not living their faith or who may not even have their children baptized or catechized. The new movements can help to promote a new evangelization to reach these people.

Many ecclesial movements and new communities go to great lengths to help their members be well inserted into

[8] Cf. *Christifideles Laici*, 30.

the liturgical and sacramental life of the Church. They thus help to reawaken vocations to Christian marriage, to the ministerial priesthood and to the consecrated life.

The ecclesial movements and new communities also motivate their members to engage in catechesis and in person-to-person presentation of the Gospel.

Some ecclesial movements and new communities promote works of mercy and charity. They take care of the homeless. They organize one hot meal a day for people in great need. They look after the sick and refugees.

Considering the large size of many parishes, the ecclesial movements and new communities can help millions of Catholics to gather in smaller units and have a deeper sense of being members of the Church in which they are brothers and sisters. They thus help individuals not to feel forgotten but rather to be known and appreciated as persons, as co-pilgrims on the way to salvation. There is no doubt that the movements and communities are gifts of the Holy Spirit to the Church in our time.

12

Formation of the Laity

If the lay faithful are to rise to the demands of their vocation and mission, they need to be prepared for it. They need adequate formation. They cannot automatically reach the desirable heights. Help and growth are necessary. Blessed John Paul II discusses formation for the lay apostolate in the last chapter of *Christifideles Laici*.

Aspects of formation

Formation can be looked at from many angles or aspects. Of priority is spiritual formation. The Christian has to be in union with Christ and to grow in that union. The reading of the Sacred Scriptures and active participation in the sacred liturgy are indispensable.

Doctrinal formation has great importance, so that the layperson knows more and more the riches of the faith and learns to love them and to integrate them with daily life and is able to give an adequate answer to those who ask about the faith that gives meaning and synthesis to his life (cf. 1 Pet 3:15). Systematic catechesis on the faith is part of doctrinal formation. In this respect, the *Catechism of the Catholic Church* and the *Compendium of the Social Doctrine of the Church* are permanent *vademecums* for the mature layperson, especially if that person is serving in the political, economic or academic domains of society. Important, too, are encyclical letters of the pope and pastoral letters of bishops that treat contemporary issues relevant to the lay apostolate at a given time.

Formation should also attend to the personal growth of the layperson in the cultivation of social virtues such as honesty, justice, sincerity, courtesy, moral courage, nobility of character and openness to dialogue. And not to be forgotten is expertise in one's own profession, since our work not only perfects us as persons, but is also our way of living and showing solidarity with our fellow citizens.

Integrated formation

Formation should help the layperson to live a life of acceptable and harmonious synthesis between duties as a Christian and duties as a citizen. Such a person's "spiritual life" and "secular life" should be lived as one life. Family, work, leisure and politics should be lived in one vital synthesis animated by the faith. "Every area of the lay faithful's lives, as different as they are, enters into the plan of God, who desires that these very areas be the 'places in time' where the love of Christ is revealed and realized for both the glory of the Father and service of others."[1]

This unity of life includes also the culture in which a layperson lives and works. Faith and life, Gospel and culture must meet and be lived in a convinced way by the well-formed layperson. Well known is the famous remark of Blessed John Paul II that "a faith that does not affect a person's culture is a faith 'not fully embraced, not entirely thought out, not faithfully lived'."[2]

---

[1] *Christifideles Laici*, 59.

[2] Ibid.; also in John Paul II, Discourse to the participants in the National Congress of Church Movements of Cultural Responsibility, January 16, 1982, 2.

Formation is an ongoing process

Nobody reaches the height of his growth in one day. Formation is an ongoing process. In matters of faith and apostolate, God's grace is indispensable. Jesus our Master teaches us: "I am the true vine, and my Father is the vinedresser. Every branch of mine that bears no fruit, he takes away, and every branch that does bear fruit he prunes, that it may bear more fruit" (Jn 15:1–2).

Christian formation is a continual process in which the individual Christian matures in the faith, becomes more like Christ, remains more and more open to the action of the Holy Spirit, and consequently lives his vocation and mission with greater authenticity. The Synod of Bishops in 1987 affirmed that "the formation of the lay faithful must be placed among the priorities of a diocese. It ought to be so placed within the plan of pastoral action that the efforts of the whole community (clergy, lay faithful and religious) converge on this goal."[3]

Pope Benedict XVI insisted that African bishops pay great attention to formation for the laity: "See to it that laypeople acquire a genuine awareness of their ecclesial mission and encourage them to engage in it with responsibility, always seeking the common good. The permanent formation programs offered to lay people, and above all to political or economic leaders, must insist on conversion as a necessary condition for the transformation of the world."[4]

---

[3] *Propositio* 40, quoted in *Christifideles Laici*, 57.
[4] *Africae Munus*, 103.

To discover and live one's vocation and mission

The main objective of formation is to help the layperson discover his vocation and mission ever more clearly and live it with increasing generosity. It is a gradual, indeed a daily, process. The individual learns each day to say to the Lord: "Speak, LORD, for your servant hears" (1 Sam 3:9).

To discover the will of the Lord for us involves listening to the word of God and the Church, praying constantly, having recourse to a wise spiritual director, and careful discernment of God's gifts to us and of the situation of the society in which we find ourselves.

Agents of formation

In the first place, it is God's grace that forms us. God's grace begins the good work in us, carries it on and brings it to a happy conclusion. God only asks us not to spoil his work but, instead, to give a little cooperation. In the *Sequence* for the Mass of Pentecost day, the Church prays to the Holy Spirit: "Light most blessed, shine on the hearts of your faithful, even into their darkest corners; for without your aid man can do nothing good, and everything is sinful." Saint Bonaventure writes that the Holy Spirit goes "to where he is loved, where he is invited, where he is awaited".[5] Every Christian who wants to grow in formation must be open to the hidden but powerful action of the Holy Spirit.

---

[5] Sermon for the IV Sunday after Easter, ed. Quaracchi, IX, p. 311, quoted by R. Cantalamessa: Third Advent Sermon, on December 16, 2011, p. 8.

Jesus Christ, our Master and Teacher, makes himself available to us through his Church. If a layperson lives in sincere fellowship in the Church with other laity, with the clergy and with religious, his formation will be an ongoing process. Saul at his conversion was helped in the faith by Ananias (cf. Acts 9:17–19). Baptized and grown to maturity in Christ, Paul in turn became God's instrument for the formation of many others in Christ.

The diocese, the parish and basic Christian communities also make their own contribution to the formation of a layperson. Fraternal collaboration is itself a school for the Gospel. We learn from others and grow in our contact with them.

The family, the Catholic school or university and the pastoral center or center for spiritual renewal each makes its own important contribution, according to the capabilities of the individual layperson who profits from it. It has already been examined above how ecclesial movements and new communities can become powerful agents of lay Christian formation and life.

Every Christian needs ongoing formation. But such formation becomes more urgent for leaders in the various lay apostolate groups or associations. "Forming those who, in turn, will be given the responsibility for the formation of the lay faithful, constitutes a basic requirement of assuring the general and widespread formation of all the lay faithful."[6] Every diocese and lay apostolate organization should bear this in mind. We must thank God for the great work that has been accomplished in this area in the Church of our times.

---

[6] *Christifideles Laici*, 63.

We marvel at the depth and magnanimity of God's grace. Jesus, in the mystery of his Church, has called all mankind to share in the wonders of the redemption. He has in his Church provided for the equal dignity of all the baptized, together with diversity and complementarity in the various apostolates that they are expected to carry out. The hope of this book is that the lay faithful will realize more and more the dignity of their calling in the Church and in the world and that they will more vigorously take on their own distinctive role. This can very fittingly become one of the ways in which the lay faithful live the Year of Faith declared by Pope Benedict XVI to be celebrated from October 2012 to November 2013.

N

Shakein Robinson
*856 350 979.
*7000